HUME'S *ENQUIRY CONCERNING HUMAN UNDERSTANDING*

Continuum Reader's Guides

Aristotle's Nicomachean Ethics – Christopher Warne

Heidegger's Being and Time – William Blattner

Hobbes' Leviathan – Laurie Bagby

Hume's Dialogues Concerning Natural Religion – Andrew Pyle

Nietzsche's Genealogy of Morals – Daniel Conway

Plato's Republic – Luke Purshouse

Wittgenstein's Tractatus Logico-Philosophicus – Roger M.White

HUME'S *ENQUIRY CONCERNING HUMAN UNDERSTANDING*
Reader's Guide

ALAN BAILEY AND DANIEL O'BRIEN

continuum

Continuum International Publishing Group
The Tower Building
11 York Road
London SE1 7NX

80 Maiden Lane
Suite 704
New York, NY 10038

British Library Cataloguing-in-Publication Data
A catalogue record for this book is available from the British Library.

ISBN 0826485081 (hardback) ISBN 082648509X (paperback)

Library of Congress Cataloging-in-Publication Data
A catalog record for this book is available from the Library of Congress

Typeset by Servis Filmsetting Ltd, Manchester
Printed and bound in Great Britain by
Cromwell Press, Trowbridge, Wiltshire

CONTENTS

CONTENTS

PREFACE

This book is a guide to what we consider to be one of the greatest works of western philosophy. The *Enquiry* has been long neglected and dismissed as a watered-down and popularized version of Hume's *Treatise of Human Nature*. Part of our motivation for writing the present book is accordingly the wish to contribute to a reassessment of the *Enquiry*: the *Enquiry* should be seen as the most developed and ambitious product of Hume's secular and naturalistic approach.

The main body of the guide consists of a step by step exposition and critique of Hume's arguments in the twelve sections that make up his *Enquiry*. We begin, however, with a little history: both personal and philosophical. Hume's life was far from the closeted life of the typical academic; and we shall discuss Hume's milieu and certain important philosophical influences on his thinking. At the end of the book we shall take a selective look at how Humean themes permeate contemporary philosophy.

References are given both to the Oxford Philosophical Texts version of the *Enquiry Concerning Human Understanding* edited by T. Beauchamp (1772) and to the version edited by Selby-Bigge and Nidditch (1777). Thus (12.16 / 155) refers to paragraph 16 of Section 12 of the Beauchamp edition and page 155 of the Selby-Bigge and Nidditch edition.

A. B.
D. O'B.
February 2006

ACKNOWLEDGEMENTS

Edward Craig's lectures on Hume's *Dialogues Concerning Natural Religion* at Cambridge helped to reinforce my early interest in Hume, and I was also fortunate enough to have been assigned John Kenyon, a formidably enthusiastic Humean, as my doctoral supervisor at Oxford. Other important personal influences on my understanding of Hume have been Marie McGinn, Galen Strawson, Bridget Clarke and Helen Steward; and I would also like to express my thanks to the following colleagues at Birmingham and Keele: Harold Noonan, Joss Walker, Iain Law, Josie D'Oro, Geraldine Coggins and Monica Mookherjee.

References within the main body of the text have deliberately been kept to a minimum. It is all the more important, therefore, to acknowledge some key literary influences at this point. The work of Richard Popkin and Robert Fogelin on the nature of Hume's scepticism and his relationship to Pyrrhonism has had a major impact on my understanding of Hume, and that influence will be evident throughout this book. Stephen Everson's work on the nature of the difference between Humean ideas and impressions has been equally influential with regard to that particular topic, and John Gaskin's writings on Hume's philosophy of religion have played a crucial role in bringing home to me the extent to which the *Enquiry* is aimed at undermining the unjustified pretensions of organized religion.

Finally, I wish to dedicate this book to Susan-Judith Hoffmann, Bridget Clarke, Paul Muench and the city of Providence, Rhode Island, for their hospitality at a crucial time in the writing process.

A.B.

ACKNOWLEDGEMENTS

My interest and admiration for Hume were kindled by the lectures of Barry Falk and Harold Noonan, and my conversations with Martin Hall have a habit of concluding with 'well, that's what Hume would say'. Thanks also to the Department of Philosophy at Birmingham, past and present, and especially to Joss Walker, Darragh Byrne, Alex Miller and Iain Law for their encouragement over the years. Parts of Chapter 5, 'Hume's Influence' are taken from O'Brien, *An Introduction to the Theory of Knowledge*, Polity Press, Cambridge, 2006.

This book is dedicated to Lucy for all those times when I didn't have time to dine and play backgammon.

D. O'B.

CHAPTER 1

THE *ENQUIRY* AND ITS CONTEXT

The case for regarding David Hume as the greatest of all British philosophers is a strong one. Certainly his only plausible rival would be John Locke (1632–1704), whose principal philosophical work, *An Essay Concerning Human Understanding*, was a remarkable attempt to reshape philosophical inquiry so as to accommodate the methods and increasing authority of the experimental science that developed in Europe over the course of the seventeenth century. The influence of the *Essay* on the intellectual climate in Britain during the hundred years or so after its publication in 1689 can scarcely be overestimated, and no one reading Hume's own writings can be in any doubt that they are the product of an author whose thinking has been profoundly shaped by both the spirit and the content of the *Essay*. But once these points have rightly been acknowledged, it nevertheless still seems true that Hume is someone who generally looks more deeply than Locke into the status and nature of philosophy as an intellectual activity. He is also the first author writing in English to provide a comprehensive articulation of a secular worldview, and his devastating critique of the design argument for the existence of a deity played a major part in breaking the grip of Christianity on educated opinion within Britain.

David Hume was born in Edinburgh on 26 April 1711; and in his brief autobiography, 'My Own Life', he is at some pains to emphasize his family's connections within Scottish society: he describes his father's family as 'a Branch of the Earl of Home's, or Hume's', and he tells us that his mother 'was Daughter of Sir David Falconer, President of the College of Justice' (1776: 611).

When he was 12, Hume enrolled as a student at the University of Edinburgh, but, like most of his contemporaries, he left university without being awarded a degree. He then half-heartedly applied himself to studying to be a lawyer. However while Hume was ostensibly perusing legal textbooks, he was primarily devoting himself to reading books dealing with philosophy and literary matters. As a result of this reading, Hume became increasingly convinced of the need to find some new method for resolving disputes in these areas of inquiry, and he reports that:

> When I was about 18 Years of Age, there seem'd to be open'd up to me a new Scene of Thought, which transported me beyond Measure, & made me with an Ardor natural to young men, throw up every other Pleasure or Business to apply entirely to it. (1993: 346)

Hume's initial efforts to develop these insights about philosophy and the other moral sciences led to a nervous breakdown. A ravenous appetite transformed him in the space of a few weeks from a thin, gangly youth into the rotund and corpulent figure familiar to us from portraits of Hume in his later years. He also found himself unable to concentrate on the task of shaping his voluminous notes and writings so as to make their sense perspicuous to potential readers. These problems persuaded Hume to seek out a more active way of life. Although he was still convinced of the importance and significance of his intellectual studies, he decided 'to lay them aside for some time, in order the more effectually to resume them' (1993: 350). Thus in 1734 he left Scotland in order to take up employment in a merchant's office in Bristol. However, this turned out to be a very unsatisfactory appointment, and Hume soon decided instead to move to France to resume his attempt at putting his philosophical ideas into a presentable form. He eventually settled in La Flèche, the town in Anjou where Descartes received his school education, and during his three years in France he wrote his first and longest philosophical work, *A Treatise of Human Nature*. Hume returned to London in 1738 in order to seek out a publisher, and Books One and Two of the *Treatise* were published anonymously in 1739. Book Three then followed in 1740.

The critical reception received by the *Treatise* was not of the kind sought by its young author. In 'My Own Life', Hume expressed his disappointment with this reception in dramatic terms:

Never literary Attempt was more unfortunate than my Treatise of human Nature. It fell *dead-born from the Press*, without reaching such distinction, as even to excite a Murmur amongst the Zealots. (1776: 612)

Hume's next literary project, however – two volumes of short essays on topics in the areas of morality and politics – was favourably reviewed, and this success reinforced Hume's determination to continue to put his ideas before the public.

In 1745, though, Hume suffered a serious personal set-back when his candidature for the vacant Chair of Ethics and Pneumatical Philosophy at the University of Edinburgh ended in failure. This persuaded him to accept a post as tutor to the Marquess of Annandale. Unfortunately, by the time Hume actually took up his duties, the Marquess had gone hopelessly insane. Not surprisingly, then, Hume lasted less than a year in this post, though he nevertheless seems to have managed to find sufficient free time from his duties to write most of the work that would subsequently become known as *An Enquiry Concerning Human Understanding*.

Hume's next post was that of a secretary to a military expedition commanded by a distant relative, Lieutenant-General James St Clair, and he took on the pensionable army rank of Judge-Advocate. At the time Britain was fighting against France as part of the War of the Austrian Succession, and this eventually led to Hume finding himself part of a British force besieging the port of Lorient in Brittany. This siege culminated in the British troops retreating back to their ships just when the French garrison had decided to surrender, and the resulting scandal back in Britain saw Hume energetically employed in writing letters and official memoranda defending his relative's reputation and judgement.

In 1748, two years after this military debacle, Hume published the book he had put together while working as a tutor. In many ways it can usefully be seen as a substantial reworking of Book One of the *Treatise*, and it was originally published under the title *Philosophical Essays Concerning Human Understanding* before being given its present title in 1757. In style, it is a marked advance on the *Treatise* as it is much more elegant and lucid. It is also very noticeable that the *Enquiry*, unlike the *Treatise*, includes explicit discussions of the rational status of religious belief. Some hostile critics of Hume have interpreted these additions as part of an opportunistic attempt at garnering literary notoriety. In reality, however, it seems clear from a letter written by Hume in 1737 that these discussions actually constitute the return of material cut from Hume's original drafts of the *Treatise* in an effort to make it more acceptable to the religiously orthodox. In this letter Hume discusses his desire to seek the opinion of Dr Joseph Butler, an Anglican bishop and highly regarded theologian, on the merits of the *Treatise*, and Hume makes the following comments about the changes he has made to the body of the text:

> I am at present castrating my work, that is, cutting off its nobler parts; that is, endeavouring that it shall give as little offence as possible, before which, I could not pretend to put it into the Doctor's hands. This is a piece of cowardice, for which I blame myself, though I believe none of my friends will blame me. (1932: 25)

Three years later, in 1751, Hume published the *Enquiry Concerning the Principles of Morals*. This too can be seen as a reworking of one of the books of the *Treatise*, in this case Book Three, and we know from 'My Own Life' that Hume regarded this *Enquiry* as 'incomparably the best' of all his writings (1776: 613). Eventually Book Two of the *Treatise* was similarly reworked, but in this case the result was less impressive. The resulting *Dissertation on the Passions* is probably the least read of Hume's substantial works, and even Hume seems to have had a low opinion of its merits.

Hume's next major literary project was his *History of England*, and he published the first volume in 1757. Within ten years the completed *History of England from the Invasion of Julius Caesar to the Glorious Revolution* became the most popular and best-selling history book published in Britain prior to Gibbon's *Decline and Fall of the Roman Empire*. This book made Hume's reputation, and it also brought in substantial amounts of money. Indeed, Hume's *History* was so influential that even in the second half of the twentieth century, the catalogues of the British Museum Library referred to Hume as a historian rather than a philosopher.

In 1763 Hume became Secretary to the British Embassy in Paris. He was a huge success in the fashionable salons of that city despite his tendency to speak French with a heavy Scottish accent. Upon Hume's return to London in 1766, he took up the post of Under-Secretary of State in the Northern Department for a year. He then gave up public office and retired to Edinburgh. At this point in his life, Hume's *Treatise* became a renewed object of critical attention. The discussions of the *Treatise* by Thomas Reid were presented in a polite and judicious manner, but the treatment meted out to the book by other critics was far more hostile. Hume's own policy was to abstain from publicly responding to such attacks, but they did persuade him to instruct his publisher in 1775 to affix an advertisement to all future editions of his collected works repudiating the *Treatise*.

Hume died of cancer on 25 August 1776. He had known for some time that his condition was incurable, and he spent the last months of his life engaged in revisions to his philosophical and historical writings. In particular, he worked on alterations to his *Dialogues Concerning Natural Religion*, which were eventually published posthumously in 1779 by his nephew. About six weeks before Hume's death, he was visited at his home in Edinburgh by James Boswell, who was eager to discover Hume's views on immortality and religion as his life drew to an end. Hume apparently said that he had never 'entertained any beleif in Religion since he began to read Locke and Clarke' (Mossner 1980: 597). Boswell also records that when he asked Hume whether it was possible that there might be a future state, Hume answered that 'it was possible that a piece of coal put upon the fire would not burn' and that 'it was a most unreasonable fancy that we should exist for ever'.

After Hume's death, his good friend Adam Smith, the economist, wrote the following assessment of his character, which was published alongside Hume's 'My Own Life' in 1777.

> Upon the whole I have always considered him, both in his lifetime and since his death, as approaching as nearly to the idea of a perfectly wise and virtuous man, as perhaps the nature of human frailty will admit. (Mossner 1980: 604)

Given the many slights directed against Hume's character and philosophical sincerity both during his life and more especially after his death, Smith's remarks provide a salutary corrective. How many of us could seriously expect to be remembered in such terms even by our closest friends?

As the content of the *Enquiry* overlaps substantially with that of the earlier and much longer *Treatise*, there has been a tendency to regard the *Treatise* as Hume's philosophical masterpiece and the *Enquiry* as little more than a truncated popularization prepared by Hume to further his pursuit of literary fame. In reality, however, there is a strong case for holding that the *Enquiry* is, in the areas it explicitly covers, the work that better represents Hume's mature philosophical vision.

Hume's own opinion on such a matter must be given considerable weight, and one forthright expression of his views can be found in the advertisement repudiating the *Treatise* that has already been mentioned. Hume drew up this advertisement or notification himself, and he instructed his publisher to place it at the start of the volume of his *Essays and Treatises on Several Subjects* that began with the *Enquiry*. It opens with the statement that 'Most of the principles, and reasonings, contained in this volume, were published in a work in three volumes, called *A Treatise of Human Nature*', and it goes on to say that the author 'not finding it successful . . . cast the whole anew in the following pieces, where some negligences in his former reasoning and more in the expression, are, he hopes, corrected' (p. 83 / 2). The advertisement then denounces critics who have chosen to take the early formulation of the author's views found in the *Treatise* as the target for their attacks, and culminates in the asseveration that: 'Henceforth, the Author desires that the following Pieces may alone be regarded as containing his philosophical sentiments and principles'.

These remarks are sometimes dismissed as the ill-tempered judgements of an exhausted invalid who had lost interest in philosophy as an activity, and was simply seeking the easiest possible way of protecting his public reputation as a literary figure and intellectual. However, Hume expressed substantially the same opinion nearly 25 years earlier in a private letter written to one of his closest friends, Gilbert Elliot of Minto, in 1751:

> I believe the philosophical Essays [i.e. the *Enquiry* under its original title] contain everything of Consequence relating to the Understanding, which you would meet with in the Treatise; & I give you my Advice against reading the latter. By shortening & simplifying the Questions, I really render them much more complete. *Addo dum minuo*. The philosophical Principles are the same in both. But I was carry'd away by the Heat of Youth & Invention to publish too precipitately. So vast an Undertaking, plan'd

before I was one and twenty, & compos'd before twenty five, must necessarily be very defective. (1932: 158)

In this latter instance, it is clear that Hume's expressed preference for the *Enquiry* was not part of a defence of his popular image: he was instead simply trying to assist a friend to comprehend his philosophical position. Moreover, this was actually a philosophically productive period of time for Hume as he was in the process of writing an initial draft of his *Dialogues Concerning Natural Religion*, a book that has a fully deserved reputation as one of the most incisive and elegant philosophical works ever written on the topic of the rational status of religious belief.

On the basis, then, that we should, whenever possible, defer to the dispassionate and reflective judgement of an author on the issue of which of his works most accurately expresses his philosophical views, we seem to be led towards some important conclusions about how we can best understand Hume's true views on those topics that are covered in both the *Treatise* and the *Enquiry*. The overwhelming presumption must be that we are required to give interpretative priority to the *Enquiry*. In particular the common practice of using the *Treatise* as a guide to Hume's position, and then appealing to a few supporting passages from the *Enquiry*, is entirely wrong-headed. If there is anything in the *Treatise* that is incompatible with what Hume says in the *Enquiry*, then the correct assumption to make is that the mature Hume came to regard those former claims as mistaken. Furthermore the fact that Hume specifically wrote the *Enquiry* to correct misunderstandings of the *Treatise* and to make it easier to understand his views means that where we find ourselves confronted by exegetical ambiguities, we should use our understanding of what Hume says in the *Enquiry* to correct our reading of what he seems to be saying in the *Treatise*.

In addition to the evidence provided by Hume's own judgement on the respective merits of the two works, the view that the *Enquiry* represents a philosophical advance over the *Treatise* seems to find significant confirmation in the way Hume has reorganized his material. Hume's account of the nature of causal inference is acknowledged today as one of the most important aspects of his overall philosophical position, and one that has major implications for all of his thinking about the rational status of beliefs concerning existence and matters of fact. In the *Treatise* this account is hidden away in a discussion of the origins of our concept of necessity, and Hume makes no special effort to explain its consequences to the reader. When we turn to the *Enquiry*, however, we find that Hume separates the two discussions and astutely gives his account of causal inference a dominant position in the work as a whole. Similarly, Hume's explicit discussion of epistemological scepticism in the *Treatise* takes the form of scattered fragments intermixed at times with lengthy discussions of apparently unrelated topics like personal identity and the immateriality of the soul. In the *Enquiry*, in contrast, Hume gathers most of this material together in one place, and he offers a detailed taxonomy of different forms of scepticism before setting out a novel account of how sceptical reflections can bring about changes in one's thinking that can plausibly be regarded as beneficial rather than intellectually disastrous. He also takes the crucial step of explicitly linking his arguments about causal inference to the case for scepticism, and this recognition of their sceptical potential enables him to edit out some relatively unconvincing arguments that had found a place in the *Treatise*.

Just as important, however, is the return of the material on religion that Hume had excised from the *Treatise*. It is only when this is given its appropriate place in the *Enquiry* that we can begin to appreciate the true extent of Hume's philosophical ambitions. Hume is certainly intensely interested in philosophy for its own sake, though it is also fair to say that he regards much of what passed for philosophy amongst his contemporaries as intellectually worthless; this is because it purports to describe the world while ignoring the evidence provided by experience and experimental methods of investigation. However if we look in an unprejudiced way at the *Enquiry* and the *Enquiry Concerning the Principles of Morals*, without insisting on using the bowdlerized *Treatise* as the touchstone for determining Hume's deepest concerns, it becomes evident that one of Hume's driving aims is to curb the influence of religion on human thought and action. Thus the *Enquiry Concerning the Principles of Morals*, for example, sets out a purely secular morality that severs issues of right and wrong from any ontological connection with the will of a divine being. It also provides an account of how human beings come to act in a moral fashion without needing to be guided by any divine revelation or restrained by the threat of divine punishment. And in the *Enquiry* itself we find a critique of the rational credentials of miracle reports, an attack on the effectiveness of the argument from design, and a defence of agnosticism and atheism against the claim that these modes of thought would undermine morality and political stability.

In many ways, then, the *Treatise* can be seen as akin to the workshop of a master armourer. Just as that workshop contains blazing furnaces, massive anvils, intricate metal-working tools and great stockpiles of components awaiting finishing and assembly, so the *Treatise* contains moments of philosophical brilliance, innovative methods for tackling philosophical problems and a mass of arguments whose implications lie relatively unexplored and unexplained. When we take into our hands a copy of the *Enquiry*, however, it is as though we are seizing hold of a perfectly balanced masterpiece of the swordsmith's art, a rapier that points directly at the most vulnerable areas of Hume's philosophical and theological opponents.

CHAPTER 2

SOURCES

We are fortunate enough to possess hand-written memoranda by Hume that record some of the thoughts inspired by his extensive reading during the period prior to the publication of the *Treatise*. And if we combine that information with what is known about the syllabus at the University of Edinburgh at the time when Hume was taking classes there, it becomes clear that the views expressed in the *Treatise* and the *Enquiry* represent a response to a widely disparate range of sources.

While studying at Edinburgh, for example, Hume was given a thorough grounding in both Latin literature and the experimental science associated in Britain with members of the Royal Society of London for the Improving of Natural Knowledge. In particular, the former classes served to introduce him to the writings of the Roman statesman and philosopher Cicero, who had been responsible for composing numerous philosophical works intended to give his con-temporaries access in Latin to the main ideas of Greek philosoph-ical authors of the Hellenistic era. Moreover, Hume's scientific education would have acquainted him with the ideas and theories of both Newton and Robert Boyle, the author of *The Sceptical Chymist* and one of the foremost experimental defenders of the corpuscular theory of matter (see Mossner 1980: 41–3 and Barfoot 1990: 160–8).

Newton published his *Philosophiae Naturalis Principia Math-ematica* in 1687, and this work rapidly established a new intellectual paradigm for investigations into the workings of the natural world. Newton's subsequent prestige and influence, especially in Britain, can scarcely be over-estimated, and Hume's own praise of Newton in *The History of England* is fulsome: 'In Newton this island may boast of having produced the greatest and rarest genius that ever arose for the ornament and instruction of the species' (1983: VI, 542).

The key intellectual achievement of Newton in the *Principia* was the unification of Kepler's laws for planetary motion and Galileo's law of falling objects into the single inverse-square law of gravitational attraction: the attractive force between two masses is directly proportional to the product of those masses, and inversely proportional to the square of the distance between them. This theory marks a major shift away from the explanatory principles underlying previous forms of mechanistic science. Descartes explains change in the motion of physical objects in terms of objects pulling and pushing against each other. Newton, however, seems quite content to suppose that his references to gravity possess genuine explanatory power even though he has no ability to supply push–pull accounts of how gravity operates.

Significantly Newton's approach provoked Leibniz and Cartesian physicists into accusing him of returning to the occult causes characteristic of the discredited Aristotelian physics. However, the salient difference between Newton's hypothesized forces and those invoked in the Aristotelian system lies in the fact that Newton's law can be expressed in quantitative terms and yields precise, testable predictions concerning physical systems.

Hume's own diagnosis of the respects in which Newton's methods and approach improved on those of his predecessors takes the following form:

Cautious in admitting no principles but such as were founded on experiment; but resolute to adopt every such principle, however new or unusual: From modesty, ignorant of his superiority above the rest of mankind; and thence less careful to accommodate his reasonings to common apprehensions. (1983: VI, 542)

The first section of these remarks might almost be seen as a characterization of Hume's own idealized self-image as a philosopher, and Newton's methodological principles exercised considerable influence on Hume's own procedures. It is, though, illuminating to note the chastening moral that Hume manages to extract even from Newton's great and acknowledged achievements:

While Newton seemed to draw off the veil from some of the mysteries of nature, he shewed at the same time the imperfections of the mechanical philosophy; and thereby restored her ultimate secrets to that obscurity, in which they ever did and ever will remain. (1983: VI, 542)

In looking for other philosophical influences exerted upon Hume, one crucial piece of evidence is provided by a letter written soon after he had finished the manuscript of the *Treatise*. In this letter Hume offers advice to his friend Michael Ramsay on the reading that would facilitate an understanding of the metaphysical aspects of the *Treatise*:

> I desire of you, if you have Leizure, to read once over La Recherche de la Verité of Pere Malebranche, the Principles of Human Knowledge by Dr Berkeley, some of the more metaphysical articles of Bailes Dictionary; such as those [. . . of] Zeno & Spinoza. Des-Cartes Meditations would also be useful but don't know if you will find it easily among your Acquaintances. (1964: 775)

There would, of course, have been no need for Hume to suggest that his friend should read Locke's *Essay*, as anyone living in Britain at that time with any philosophical interests whatsoever would have been familiar with the views expressed in that particular work. So we can conclude that the principal mainstream philosophers providing the intellectual background to Book One of the *Treatise*, and hence the background to the *Enquiry*, were Locke, Malebranche, Berkeley, Bayle and Descartes.

One of the key characteristics of Locke's philosophical stance was his conceptual empiricism: all of the materials of human thought, or, in Locke's favoured terminology, 'ideas', are derived from outer sensory experience or our awareness of the inner workings of our minds. Hence he rejected the supposition that we possess any innate ideas, ideas that exist in us prior to experience. This conceptual empiricism was combined with a realist view of the world and a representative theory of perception. Locke subscribed to the corpuscular theory which maintains that the real essence of a physical object lies in the inner constitution of atoms that generates its observable properties. However, he held that human senses are incapable of revealing this structure even when supplemented by such artificial aids as microscopes. Moreover, he took the view that even when we are concerned with the macrophysical properties of such objects as rocks, trees and tables, we perceive these properties and objects only indirectly by means of our direct, non-mediated awareness of ideas in our mind.

Hume shares Locke's conceptual empiricism and the emphasis on the operation of the senses as the source of our beliefs about the world. It also seems correct to describe Hume as espousing a realist view about the existence of a mind-independent physical world. However, Hume's epistemological stance appears to be radically dissimilar to Locke's. Locke is content to suppose that our beliefs about the existence and properties of physical objects are often beliefs that possess a high degree of rational justification: they are beliefs that it is much more reasonable to accept than to deny. Hume, in contrast, regards their epistemic status as much more problematic. In fact, it will emerge in the course of the *Enquiry* that Hume is inclined to hold that although these beliefs are psychologically inescapable, they are not beliefs that qualify as rationally justified.

The inclusion of Descartes on Hume's list of recommended reading is perhaps best understood as providing a salient example of the kind of approach to philosophy that Hume wished to undermine. Descartes' philosophical system relied upon a priori intuitions about the nature of causality that Hume's thoroughgoing empiricism entirely eschews. Furthermore, Descartes placed the human mind entirely outside the natural order: not only were such minds supposed to be non-physical substances, but they were also presented as lying beyond the reach of causal necessitation. Human actions manifest a kind of freedom that cannot be found anywhere in the physical world or in the behaviour of animals.

In the case of Berkeley and Malebranche, the influence on Hume is somewhat more positive. In the final section of the *Enquiry*, Hume explicitly appeals to some of Berkeley's arguments about the kind of general ideas that can be formed by the human mind. And there are striking similarities between Malebranche's views about the imagination and Hume's own account of how human beings form beliefs about matters of fact. Malebranche placed great emphasis on the claim that if two ideas are repeatedly conjoined in experience, then the imagination eventually comes to link these ideas together so closely that the presence of one of these ideas will automatically bring the other into our mind, even if we have no good reason for supposing that the objects or properties represented by those ideas are genuinely linked together. In the *Enquiry* an identical associative mechanism is given a vital role in Hume's explanation of how we come to make and endorse causal inferences.

It is striking, however, that the influence of both Berkeley and Malebranche on Hume's views appears to have been primarily a matter of reinforcing his epistemological pessimism. Hume's appeal to Berkeley occurs in the context of a discussion of whether physical objects exist independently of the mind; Hume concludes that their doing so is 'contrary to reason; at least, if it be a principle of reason, that all sensible qualities are in the mind, not in the object' (12.16 / 155). And, in a footnote to this discussion, Hume says:

> This argument is drawn from Dr. BERKELEY; and indeed most of the writings of that very ingenious author form the best lessons of scepticism, which are to be found either among the ancient or modern philosophers, BAYLE not excepted. (12.15, fn. 32 / 155, fn.1)

Hume accepts that Berkeley genuinely thought of himself as attempting to argue against scepticism. However, Hume sees Berkeley's idealism – the claim that objects such as trees and rocks are ultimately nothing more or less than collections of mind-dependent ideas – as having a negative epistemological impact. In Hume's judgement, Berkeley fails to provide good reasons for accepting his conclusions, but his arguments still serve to bring to our attention an immaterialist hypothesis that is both diametrically opposed to our ordinary common-sense beliefs and impervious to rational refutation.

Malebranche too seems to have been seen by Hume as offering a challenge to common sense that it lacks the capacity to overcome, even when assisted by the resources of philosophy. Malebranche sought to exhibit the associative tendencies of the imagination as a pervasive source of false beliefs. Hume, however, gives this view a distinctive twist by presenting these tendencies as the connecting principles for all our ideas (see Section 3 of the *Enquiry*) and arguing that they form the foundation for all our beliefs about matters of fact that go beyond the evidence of our present experiences and memories (see Sections 4 and 5). By extending the supposed influence of the association of ideas in this way, Hume deprives us of the comforting thought that we sometimes have access to a more trustworthy means of forming such beliefs. He also does nothing at all to mitigate the impact of Malebranche's numerous examples of where the association of ideas leads to false or unjustified beliefs. The end result is that we are led to think of our empirical inferences as inextricably bound up with the operations of a mental mechanism whose credentials as a source of justification are deeply flawed.

Turning, then, to the remaining name on Hume's list, Pierre Bayle, we encounter someone who seems to have influenced Hume both through his own views and by drawing Hume's attention to the philosophical stance known as Pyrrhonean scepticism. The fullest extant exposition of this stance can be found in the surviving works of Sextus Empiricus, who was head of this particular school of scepticism around the end of the second century AD. A reference to Sextus' writings in Hume's *Enquiry Concerning the Principles of Morals* strongly suggests that Hume had read some Sextus by the time he composed that book (see 1777: 180, fn. 1), but there is no evidence that he had any first-hand acquaintance with Sextus' writings at the time when he was writing the earlier *Enquiry Concerning Human Understanding*. However, he does discuss this form of scepticism by name in the final section of the *Enquiry*, and his remarks there seem to be consistent with the account Bayle gives of Pyrrhonean scepticism in the article 'Pyrrho' which is included in his *Historical and Critical Dictionary* (see 1991: 194–209).

Perhaps the most conspicuous feature of Bayle's own philosophical discussions was his repeated failure to take up definite positions. Although he considered at great length in the *Dictionary* such issues as materialism, the physical continuum, and whether animals have souls, he concluded again and again that reason could not provide any stable and intellectually satisfactory answers to such conundrums. And this seems to have been the point of these intricate discussions: he hoped that his readers would become increasingly disillusioned with reason by being exposed to endless examples of how it initially points one way and then, with a little ingenuity, comes to point briefly in some opposite direction before the whole process is put in motion again. Of course this invites the question of what serves as the source of Bayle's own beliefs given his apparent lack of confidence in reason. In the case of religion, Bayle was insistent that our beliefs must be founded on faith and God's grace; and, in respect of our other beliefs, Bayle accorded a role to such non-rational considerations as 'the force of education . . . and, even if you wish, ignorance and the natural inclination to reach decisions' (1991: 195). As we shall see, 'natural inclination' also plays a key role in Hume's account of belief formation.

CHAPTER 3

OVERVIEW OF THEMES

1. EMPIRICISM

Hume undeniably qualifies as some kind of empiricist because of the emphasis he places on experience as a source of both our concepts and our beliefs. At the conceptual level Hume appears to have remained broadly within the tradition represented by Locke. Thus Hume is happy enough in Section 2 of the *Enquiry* to reaffirm and defend the view that all our materials of thought are derived from sense perception or our awareness of our inner sentiments. Moreover, Hume explicitly maintains that this view guides us towards a way of clarifying the meaning of the linguistic terms we employ. Whereas our ideas are often faint and confused, the impressions from which they are ultimately derived are 'strong and vivid' (2.9 / 22). Hume therefore suggests that if we are unclear about the idea or ideas associated with a particular term, then we can clarify this matter by tracing these ideas back to their source in sense perception or our primary passions.

Hume does not, though, regard experience as capable of conferring a positive degree of justification on beliefs about matters of fact. Moreover, he definitely does not regard a priori reasoning as an alternative means of justifying such beliefs. Consequently one of the initially puzzling aspects of Hume's philosophical approach is its marked lack of justificatory resources. Whereas most philosophers are concerned to exhibit their beliefs as rationally justified even if they are diffident about presenting them as certainly true, Hume frequently gives the impression of being someone who is enthusiastically exposing the deficiencies in the justification of both other people's beliefs and his own. At the same time Hume often seems conspicuously unconcerned about this lack of justification: at points where we might naturally expect him to say that these unjustified beliefs ought to be given up, he tends to talk instead about their indispensability and psychological inevitability. And it is here that we encounter another element of Hume's empiricism, an element that can appropriately be called his doxastic empiricism.

Most people, including philosophers, assume that if we lose our confidence in the justification of a particular belief, then we are under some kind of intellectual obligation to discard that belief until such time as we can find some rational justification for holding it to be true. Hume, in contrast, appears to be intent on severing the link between viewing a belief as one that it is appropriate to hold, and viewing it as a rationally justified belief. In Section 5, for example, Hume argues his way to the conclusion that:

> Even after we have experience of the operations of cause and effect, our conclusions from that experience are *not* founded on reasoning, or any process of the understanding. (4.15 / 32)

This conclusion, however, does not lead Hume to recommend that we should refrain from causal reasoning. Instead he devotes himself to reassuring us that his critique of such reasoning will be unable to disrupt our practice of making such inferences. And the same striking pattern of thought is exhibited repeatedly in the final section of the *Enquiry*: a challenge to the rational status of a pervasive class of beliefs is examined and then seemingly endorsed before Hume goes on to maintain that neither he nor anyone else is in danger of abandoning these particular beliefs.

Significantly this stability of belief in the face of these negative reflections is ascribed by Hume to custom and experience. Perception automatically and irresistibly generates beliefs in the mind-independent existence of physical objects (12.7 / 151). And the causal reasoning that generates beliefs about objects that we have not yet perceived is presented by Hume as a 'species of instinct or mechanical power, that acts in us unknown to ourselves' (9.6 / 108), and this is put into motion by repeated observations of objects of one kind being followed or accompanied by objects of another specific type (see 5.20 / 54 and 12.22 / 159). For Hume, therefore, the senses might not have the justificatory powers ascribed to them by those thinkers who embrace epistemological empiricism; he does, however, regard them as having an ability to generate and sustain beliefs about matters of fact that is far more potent than any possible rival source of conviction.

2. EPISTEMOLOGICAL SCEPTICISM

Present-day discussions of epistemological scepticism tend to be unduly influenced by the mistaken supposition that the protagonist of Descartes' 'First Meditation' is a paradigm instance of someone who uses sceptical arguments to arrive at a sceptical conclusion about the status of our beliefs about the world. The dominance of this picture of what supposedly constitutes a sceptical outlook is particularly unfortunate when it comes to arriving at an accurate understanding of Hume's philosophical stance in the *Enquiry*. Even a relatively cursory examination of what Hume says in this work rightly convinces people that he cannot coherently be thought of as a sceptic along Cartesian lines. And when this conclusion is combined with the observation that Hume offers some vigorous criticisms of what he refers to as 'PYRRHONISM or the excessive principles of scepticism' (12.21 / 158), it is often supposed that this is sufficient to establish that Hume is not any kind of radical sceptic at all.

The claim that Hume is not a sceptic of the kind described by Descartes is plainly a sound judgement. Descartes regards suspension of belief as being under the control of the will except in cases where we are presented with a clear and a distinct perception that p, and in those cases we actually have a decisively good reason for taking it to be true that p. Similarly, Descartes deploys sceptical arguments in a context where it is presupposed that we have a normative obligation to suspend belief, at least temporarily, if we uncover any grounds for doubting that it is true that p. And, for Descartes, such grounds for doubt are seen as calling into question the certainty of our beliefs rather than their rationality. If anyone were to press the question of what entitles the Cartesian meditator to suppose that his negative epistemological arguments possess true premises and rely on valid inferential principles, Descartes would give the straightforward reply that the meditator is free to regard himself as having a positive level of (a priori) justification for endorsing those premises and principles.

In contrast, Hume's critique of the epistemic status of our beliefs seems primarily to bear not on the question of whether they are known to be true, but on the question of whether they possess any positive degree of justification. Someone who says, as Hume does, that our causal conclusions 'are *not* founded on reasoning, or any process of the understanding' (4.15 / 32) cannot plausibly be interpreted as merely making the modest point that these conclusions are not known to be true. If that remark has any sceptical import whatsoever, it calls into question not just our supposed knowledge, but also the supposition that these conclusions are better justified than some set of contrary conclusions. Moreover, in the final section of the *Enquiry* Hume describes sceptics as engaged in an attempt to destroy '*reason* by argument and ratiocination' (12.17 / 155), and his subsequent discussion makes it clear that he regards the target of their attack as encompassing both a priori and empirical reasoning. He says that the sceptic's critique 'shows his force or rather his and our weakness; and seems, for the time at least, to destroy all assurance and conviction' (12.22 / 159). And assurance and conviction are not restored by diagnosing some flaw in the sceptic's *arguments*, but rather by the fact that it is psychologically impossible for his doubts and scruples to be sustained in the face of the lively perceptions that come flooding in as soon as we turn our attention to the real objects in our immediate environment.

Moreover, as we have just seen, Hume plainly does not share the Cartesian belief that we can always suspend judgement when we do not have good reasons for embracing a belief as true. The sceptic's arguments ultimately fail because we are psychologically incapable of maintaining a universal suspension of judgement about such matters. The sceptic's arguments may be excellent examples of their type, and it may be true that they cannot be refuted by further arguments, but neither they nor the human will have the causal power to dislodge the beliefs implanted in us by perception and the unreflective instincts and mechanisms that drive forward our common-sense inferences. As Hume explains to us: 'Nature is always too strong for principle' (12.23 / 160).

It also seems clear that Hume does not see this failure on our part to suspend judgement in response to sceptical arguments as a breach of one of our fundamental obligations. Indeed he tends to portray the results of such suspension of judgement, if it could be achieved, as utterly disastrous (see, in particular, 12.23 / 160). If we were to wish to continue to think of ourselves as essentially rational doxastic agents, then we would be acting in bad faith if we simply ignored sceptical arguments or pretended that we could refute them. However, if we honestly confess that we cannot arrive at rationally justified beliefs, we are free to give ourselves over without self-reproach to the guidance of the belief-forming mechanisms that form part of our basic humanity.

It emerges, then, that Hume's philosophical position appears to be far more similar to the Pyrrhonean scepticism espoused by Sextus Empiricus than we might initially have suspected from Hume's attempts to disassociate himself from that stance. Sextus too makes liberal use of arguments, such as Agrippa's five tropes, that attack not just the supposition that we have knowledge but rather the supposition that our beliefs are any better justified than contrary beliefs (see 1933: I, 164–77). Moreover, although Sextus does describe the Pyrrhonist as suspending judgement on a wide range of topics, he does not present this as a matter of the Pyrrhonist responding to an intellectual obligation (see, for example, 1933: I, 19, 123, and 196). Instead it is something that is supposed to be psychologically forced upon the Pyrrhonist when he recognizes the lack of justification possessed by the great majority of his beliefs. The Pyrrhonist simply responds passively to this psychological constraint. Equally Sextus does seem to accept that the Pyrrhonist retains some beliefs, officially beliefs about how things phenomenologically appear to him, even after he has absorbed the full implications of his own epistemological arguments (1933: I, 19). It is again the case, though, that this is supposed to be a matter of psychological necessitation (1933: I, 19, 22, and 193). Beliefs about phenomenological appearances are no more securely justified than beliefs about matters of objective fact in the face of arguments as radical as Agrippa's tropes. They do, however, turn out to be psychologically more stable.

Now that we have noted these similarities, we are in a good position to reflect upon the exact nature of Hume's criticisms of Pyrrhonean scepticism in the *Enquiry*. Hume does not claim that these sceptical arguments are invalid. His attack is primarily directed against the claim that it is psychologically possible to suspend one's judgement about matters of objective fact, and that any such suspension could bring benefits to the thinker. Thus it is tempting to view Hume as akin to a Pyrrhonist with a more cautious view about the real-life psychological possibilities for human beings. And that, in turn, might lead us to speculate that Hume's polemic against Pyrrhonism is, in part, a tactical manoeuvre. He is making his views about justification and belief look less challenging and radical by contrasting his supposedly more moderate position with the wild and fanciful speculations of the ancient Pyrrhonists.

3. A NATURALISTIC ACCOUNT OF HUMAN BEINGS

At the time when Hume was writing the *Enquiry*, it was commonplace to regard human beings as possessing powers and capabilities that could not be explained in scientific terms. One of the sources of this view was undoubtedly the religious doctrine that man is made in God's image. It would be arrogant in the extreme to suppose that God's nature could be analysed and laid bare by the investigative methods employed by scientists (or 'natural philosophers' as they were generally known in this era). Thus, if important aspects of our human nature are ones we share in some diluted way with God, it seems legitimate to conclude that those aspects will for ever lie beyond the reach of the kind of understanding we can hope to attain in respect of systems made up of moving pieces of matter.

Another important source of such thoughts about human beings came from attempts to apply purely physical explanations to human performances. It was thought that such explanations needed to be couched in terms of pieces of matter pushing against and giving motion to other pieces of matter. Only the most optimistic of theorists would therefore have regarded themselves as having any serious chance of explaining such human activities as inferential reasoning and the intelligent use of language in physical terms.

Hume, however, is diametrically opposed to regarding human beings as exceptions to the natural order in this way. He makes no obvious challenge to the thought that the human mind has a non-physical component, but he does exploit Newton's more liberal understanding of what constitutes an acceptable scientific explanation. Hume constructs a quasi-mechanical account of how mental entities like thoughts and the products of sense perception interact to produce adaptive behaviour and intelligent reasoning. In Section 3 of the *Enquiry* he specifies certain principles of association that describe the regular causal interactions of our ideas, and in Section 5 these principles are specifically put to work to explain the process by means of which we project into the future past patterns of observed events and form beliefs accordingly. Essentially, then, he offers an account of a process that allows intelligence to emerge from a set of interactions between mental entities that are them-selves incapable of forethought and planning.

The implications of this approach to understanding the human mind turn out to be extremely far-reaching. One consequence is that it suggests that there might be no fundamental distinction between the human mind and the minds possessed by animals. In the fre-quently neglected section of the *Enquiry* entitled 'Of the Reason of Animals', Hume maintains that both humans and animals make inferences about matters of fact in accordance with exactly the same principle of custom or habit. The superiority of human reasoning in this area is presented as a matter of degree rather than as the result of human beings having access to some radically different intellec-tual faculty.

Such a naturalistic account also makes it possible to view human beings as deterministic systems. Hume argues at considerable length in Section 8 that our observations of human behaviour, and the introspectible contents of the human mind, make it just as plausible to suppose that human actions are causally determined as it is to suppose that this is true of purely physical systems. Such a doctrine might be thought to take away human liberty and undermine all ascriptions of blame and moral responsibility. Hume, however, attempts to alleviate this worry by providing an account of what is meant by talk about liberty that attempts to show that we can still qualify as acting freely even when all our actions are entirely deter-mined by a chain of events that predates our existence.

4. SECULARISM

One of the most striking features of Hume's position, given the fact that he was an eighteenth-century author rather than someone writing today, is the absence of any appeals to God's agency as an explanatory hypothesis. And, in Sections 10 and 11, Hume argues that the usual arguments in favour of the existence of the Christian God are unfounded.

Hume's approach here often causes considerable confusion to readers who are attempting to integrate it with his apparently scept-ical outlook. If we concentrate on his attitude towards the argument from design – the claim that the order manifest in the world indicates the existence of a designer with a special concern for us (Section 11) – it is tempting to read Hume as strongly implying that we would be better justified in concluding that any such designer is actually indifferent to our welfare. However, a radical epistemological sceptic would seem to be in no position to classify the latter conclusion as better justified than the former: such a sceptic would appear to be committed to finding both conclusions equally lacking in rational justification.

The key to understanding Hume here is to see him as taking up two very different perspectives at different points in the *Enquiry*. At some points he is addressing himself to the question of what it is appropriate to say about the justification of our beliefs when we are considering them from a dispassionate philosophical perspective. However, Hume is also aware that few of our beliefs can be changed permanently by the results of such consideration. Even if we make long-term changes to our assessment of the epistemic status of our beliefs, the underlying first-order beliefs are seldom affected for long. It is one thing to give up the belief that our first-order belief that trees exist is rationally justified, but it is quite another thing to suspend judgement on the existence of the trees themselves. General sceptical arguments are causally incapable of inducing us to abandon more than momentarily the belief that trees exist.

Thus, in order to engage effectively with the causes of Christian belief in an intelligent and caring designer, Hume needs to move away from the dispassionate philosophical perspective so that he is drawing people's attention to the implications of their non-sceptical commitments. Hume therefore argues that when judged according to the standards that tend to guide us in everyday life, the argument from design is a poor piece of reasoning and one with flaws that are sufficient, when fully exposed, to reduce radically the persuasiveness it sometimes manages to exert over the unwary.

A very similar pattern of argument can also be found in Hume's discussion of the evidential value of miracle reports (Section 10). Hume is aware that many religious believers found their faith on alleged miracles and supposedly fulfilled prophecies. Hume's response to this is to argue that the canons of causal reasoning to which we normally defer in the course of everyday life actually tell strongly against the belief that any of these reports of miracles and accurate prophecies are true.

This has led some hostile commentators to accuse him of inconsistency on the grounds that such a conclusion is incompatible with his scepticism about causal reasoning, and yet other commentators have inferred that we misunderstand Hume if we think of him as a radical sceptic in respect of causal reasoning (given his seeming acceptance of such reasoning in everyday life). In reality, however, it seems perfectly possible to think of Hume as immersing himself in different perspectives depending upon the needs of the moment. When Hume is speaking from the perspective of abstract philosophical reasoning, he would accept the conclusion that causal reasoning and arguments from miracle reports are both incapable of conferring any justification on their conclusions. But when he takes on the perspective of a non-sceptical participant in everyday life, our everyday epistemic standards provide reasons for rejecting the truth of miracle reports, although not for rejecting causal reasoning per se. Hume's aim, then, in his arguments against religious belief, is to draw attention to considerations that will set our everyday, natural belief-forming mechanisms moving in a direction that will subvert any inclination to find miracle reports at all persuasive.

CHAPTER 4

READING THE TEXT

1. OF THE DIFFERENT SPECIES OF PHILOSOPHY

Hume begins the *Enquiry* by drawing a distinction between two radically different ways of thinking that can both be regarded as falling
under the heading of 'moral philosophy, or the science of human
nature' (1.1 / 5). The first of these concentrates on shaping human
actions, and seeks to motivate people to act in accordance with
accepted standards of virtue and probity. The other mode of moral
philosophy, in contrast, seeks to improve our understanding of
human nature rather than our ethical character. It accordingly scrutinizes the workings of the human mind in a dispassionate and
meticulous manner in order to uncover the principles that underlie
our judgements and determine our sentiments and passions.
Moreover, this 'accurate and abstruse' (1.3 / 6) form of philosophy
seeks to achieve this goal by subsuming specific instances and
narrow regularities under more general principles. It ultimately
arrives at a grasp of those fundamental regularities that lie at the
farthest attainable limits of explanation and understanding.

Hume is under no illusions about where most people's preferences
will lie if asked to choose between these two types of philosophy. He
admits that the 'easy and obvious' philosophy that devotes itself to
the encouragement of virtuous action and generous sentiments will
enjoy the support of the majority of mankind. Many of its advocates
will maintain that it is to be preferred as both more agreeable and
more useful than abstruse philosophical reflection (1.3 / 6). As it
exploits and builds upon motives and inclinations that are frequently
in play in everyday life, this easy philosophy visibly reforms people's
conduct and shapes their character so that they come closer to the

moral ideals it recommends. In contrast, most people are inclined to suppose that no durable benefits can accrue from abstruse philosophy. It appears to be rooted in a mental disposition that is incompatible with engagement in practical matters and dissipates as soon as the philosopher ventures outside the seclusion of his library or study.

Hume further develops this theme by reminding his readers of the common supposition that human beings have a three-fold nature: as well as being reasonable beings, we are also sociable and active beings. Experience apparently shows us that we are not always in a disposition that permits us to enjoy the pleasures of company and social interaction. Similarly, the mind cannot indefinitely sustain an interest in the practicalities of work and enterprise. At times, therefore, it is natural for us to indulge our curiosity by reflecting on more speculative and theoretical topics. However, Hume suggests that although nothing is 'deemed a surer sign of an illiberal genius in an age and nation where the sciences flourish, than to be entirely destitute of all relish for those noble entertainments' (1.5 / 8), it is generally supposed that the limits of human understanding are sufficiently narrow that we cannot reasonably expect to make much progress when we devote ourselves to theoretical investigations and system-building. Thus the majority opinion is that we should engage in a mixed kind of life in which our taste for speculative thought is primarily met by philosophical attempts to illuminate the advantages and merit of a virtuous character. Abstract and profound philosophy, however, is seen as bringing with it unwelcome and discouraging consequences. Dedicating oneself to intellectual activities of this latter kind is thought to be punished:

> By the pensive melancholy which they introduce, by the endless uncertainty in which they involve you, and by the cold reception which your pretended discoveries will meet with, when communicated. (1.6 / 9)

It is therefore philosophy of the easy and obvious kind that has a place in a well-rounded life, but it is essential to keep in mind the following injunction: 'Be a philosopher; but amidst all your philosophy, be still a man' (1.6 / 9).

The highly quotable nature of that injunction, and the way it coheres with some conspicuous aspects of Hume's own approach to philosophy, have led a surprising number of commentators to treat its appearance at this particular point in the *Enquiry* as an expression of his personal views. Now it does have to be admitted that claims made by Hume in subsequent sections of the *Enquiry* suggest quite strongly that the attempt to substitute the deliverances of philosophical investigation for our pre-reflective, common-sense beliefs is frequently a futile and counter-productive undertaking. Abstruse philosophical reasoning is impotent in the face of the psychological mechanisms that bring about and sustain our everyday beliefs. And that stance is one that could potentially be summed up in aphoristic form by the injunction under consideration here. However, it seems clear that Hume responds to this recommendation in the remaining portion of the first section of the *Enquiry* by distancing himself from it.

If advocates of easy and obvious philosophy refrained from belittling the value of abstract and profound philosophy, Hume would have no objection to leaving the choice between these two forms of philosophy to personal taste. Unfortunately the matter frequently takes a more acrimonious turn, and it is often suggested that 'all profound reasonings, or what is commonly called *metaphysics*' should be dismissed as wholly devoid of value (1.7 / 9). Hume accordingly attempts to rebut this extreme view by examining what can be said in defence of reasoning of this latter kind.

Hume first identifies two related advantages. In his judgement, abstract philosophy underpins philosophy of the easy kind by providing it with the information that it needs in order to be carried out well. Hume's main analogy here is with the relationship between the painter and the anatomist. The anatomist delves into the innermost structures of the human body and he often presents for our examination seemingly repulsive and hideous objects. Nevertheless the anatomist's activities are useful to the painter whenever he attempts to produce a realistic portrait of a human figure.

> While the latter employs all the richest colours of his art, and gives his figures the most graceful and engaging airs; he must still carry his attention to the inward structure of the human body, the position of the muscles, the fabric of the bones, and the use and figure of every part or organ. (1.8 / 10)

Similarly, the easy philosophy will become more sure footed and convincing if it pays attention to what abstract philosophy can uncover about the faculties and inner workings of the human mind. Moreover, a spirit of accuracy and exactness, however it arises, is of considerable value in a wide variety of arts and professions. Thus Hume suggests that the example set by those who pursue abstract philosophical research helps to generate a similar concern with accuracy and precise thought amongst such diverse people as politicians, lawyers and generals.

Hume also maintains that even if it were true that there is nothing to be gained from abstract philosophy 'beyond the gratification of an innocent curiosity', this would still be a valuable outcome (1.10 / 11). He asserts that any 'accession to those few safe and harmless pleasures, which are bestowed on human race' is to be welcomed, and he adds that although most people may indeed find abstract philosophy too exacting to be genuinely enjoyable, there are some minds:

> Which, being endowed with vigorous and florid health, require severe exercise, and reap a pleasure from what, to the generality of mankind, may seem burdensome and laborious. (1.10 / 11)

Having brought these initial considerations to our attention, Hume then introduces us to the most pointed and polemically charged component of his defence of abstract philosophy. He concedes that the obscurity of the topics investigated by such philosophy makes it particularly susceptible to uncertainty and error. But these errors, once they have taken hold, provide a cover and a refuge for popular superstitions.

> Chaced from the open country, these robbers fly into the forest, and lie in wait to break in upon every unguarded avenue of the mind, and overwhelm it with religious fears and prejudices. The stoutest antagonist, if he remit his watch a moment, is oppressed. And many, through cowardice and folly, open the gates to the enemies, and willingly receive them with reverence and submission, as their legal sovereigns. (1.11 / 11)

From Hume's perspective, it is accordingly essential that the 'intangling brambles' which provide undeserved protection for oppressive forms of religion and political organization should be cleared away. Such brambles may have arisen in the first place from poorly directed attempts at abstract philosophy. But now that they are in existence and flourishing, only abstract philosophy can offer us any hope of eradicating them: we need to 'cultivate true metaphysics with some care, in order to destroy the false and adulterate' (1.12 / 12).

Ingeniously, then, Hume has transformed one of the principal problems with abstract philosophy into a strong motive for pursuing it with even greater determination and exactness. Of course, it might be objected at this point that it would actually be safer and more straightforward to keep away from abstract philosophy altogether; and it is worth noting that Hume himself is prepared to accept that indolence 'affords a safeguard against this deceitful philosophy' for some people (1.12 / 12). However, in the case of other people such indolence is often overbalanced by natural curiosity, and the other weakness of this supposed remedy is that it leaves untouched the metaphysical confusions and obscurities that have already arisen. And Hume sees a particular danger here. Indolence with regard to abstract philosophy may indeed be commonplace when that philosophy is presented in isolation from other forms of thought that engage our attention more readily. Nevertheless religious super-stition and political radicalism do appeal to powerful and deep-rooted passions that can readily motivate us into rash and dangerous actions. Consequently a mix of metaphysics with religion or some political doctrine can easily gain our attention. In that situation, we once again find ourselves faced with the problem that the metaphys-ical component of the mixture often obstructs our capacity to rec-ognize the dangers and errors embodied in religion and politics. Hume accordingly draws the following conclusion:

> Accurate and just reasoning is the only catholic remedy, fitted for all persons and all dispositions; and is alone able to subvert that abstruse philosophy and metaphysical jargon, which, being mixed up with popular superstition, renders it in a manner impenetrable to careless reasoners, and gives it the air of science and wisdom. (1.12 / 12)

Once the crucial importance of this negative benefit has been driven home to the reader, Hume returns to his account of the positive ben-efits of abstract philosophy. At the very least, it can provide us with a 'mental geography, or delineation of the distinct parts and powers of the mind' (1.13 / 13), one that is suitable, as we have seen, for assisting the development of the easy and obvious philosophy. And Hume makes the interesting observation here that there can be no suspicion that this mental geography is 'uncertain and chimerical' unless 'we should entertain such a scepticism as is entirely subversive of all speculation, and even action' (1.14 / 13). However, Hume also suggests that we might well be able to go further than this and generate some account of the general principles underlying mental phenomena in much the same way as natural philosophers have formulated certain physical laws of nature.

This first section of the *Enquiry* then concludes with some remarks about Hume's desire to unite the style of the easy philosophy with the more profound content of abstract philosophy. Hume readily admits that when dealing with difficult topics of inquiry, we should seek to minimize problems of comprehension and understanding by developing an accessible style that concentrates on matters of importance while avoiding unnecessary detail. Thus he endeavours to reassure the reader that in the subsequent sections of the *Enquiry* he has attempted, to the best of his ability, to 'unite the boundaries of the different species of philosophy, by reconciling profound enquiry with clearness, and truth with novelty!' (1.17 / 16).

It seems clear, therefore, that the message that Hume is trying to convey to the prospective reader is a complex one that offers a multiplicity of hints about the nature of what is to come later in the book. However, at least some of those hints will turn out to be pieces of ingenious misdirection. Some of the views Hume advances and defends in the *Enquiry* would have been instantly rejected by the overwhelming majority of his contemporaries if he had simply put these views before them in a direct manner. Consequently Hume's desire to make converts to those views persuades him to disguise some of his ultimate objectives. He must first prepare the way for a more receptive examination of their merits by introducing, in apparently non-threatening contexts, many of the modes of reasoning that will eventually be deployed in support of some distinctly unpopular conclusions.

Hume represents himself as undertaking a philosophically important and practically significant project within the framework of a book that conscientiously aims at a level of accessibility more often associated with the 'easy' philosophy. A major advantage of such an approach for Hume is that it widens the potential audience for his philosophical views. Despite Hume's lightness of touch and self-deprecating good humour in the *Enquiry* and his other post-*Treatise* writings, he is deeply committed to the idea that things would go better in society if more people could be persuaded to share his own philosophical outlook. However, he also believes that writing clearly and accessibly assists him in clarifying his own thoughts and identifying potential errors in his reasoning. And Hume, unlike many philosophers, is not simply seeking an audience that will passively receive instruction from its supposed intellectual superiors. Hume holds that when philosophy is shut up in colleges and the studies of solitary scholars, it is deprived of an essential source of guidance and relevant experience:

> Even Philosophy went to Wrack by this moaping recluse Method of Study, and became as chimerical in her Conclusions as she was unintelligible in her Stile and Manner of Delivery. And indeed, what cou'd be expected from Men who never consulted Experience in any of their Reasonings, or who never search'd for that Experience, where alone it is to be found, in common Life and Conversation. (1987: 534–5)

Hume, in part at least, is keen to attract the interest of people who do not think of themselves as expert philosophers. Their input can help to challenge some of the more absurd manifestations of philosophical inquiry and can provide crucial confirmatory evidence for philosophical theories of a more judicious kind.

A less straightforward reading, however, needs to be applied to Hume's comments about the utility of abstract metaphysics for combating the pernicious effects of popular superstition. At the time when Hume was writing the *Enquiry*, the phrase 'popular superstition' was widely used by Scottish and English writers to refer to the theological doctrines associated with Catholicism. Given, then, that most of Hume's readers would have regarded themselves as Protestants, they would undoubtedly have been encouraged by Hume's comments to suppose that the *Enquiry* would offer support to their religious views and a destructive critique of the philosophical underpinnings of rival Catholic doctrines. In reality, however, Hume's ensuing discussions offer no comfort to any form of Christianity or indeed any religion that believes in the existence of a deity concerned with human welfare and conduct. It will become clear as the *Enquiry* progresses that Hume has employed the tactical subterfuge of assembling, and presenting for his readers' endorsement, the materials for a wide-ranging critique of religious thinking while implying to those same readers that only a very restricted set of religious doctrines, doctrines indeed that very few of them would hold, are going to be the objects of attack. No doubt many of Hume's less religiously orthodox readers would have seen through this relatively thin disguise as soon as they encountered its first manifestations, and it was probably Hume's intention that they should do so. However, there is no doubt that if one wants to persuade people out of a position to which they are firmly committed, then the device of arguing for a contrary stance on the basis of premises that they have endorsed, when they thought that the real object of criticism was some set of views that they too thought were dangerously mistaken, is a very effective way of making it psychologically difficult for them to evade the force of the criticisms of their own position.

Significantly there are at least some signs of a similar tactic being employed in Hume's comments about scepticism in this section of the *Enquiry*. We have already noted that Hume holds before his reader the prospect that abstract philosophy will at least be able to tabulate accurately the powers and faculties of the human mind. And it will also be recalled that Hume asserts that its power to achieve this can only be doubted by someone prepared to embrace an extreme form of scepticism. At first sight Hume seems to be implying both that no extreme form of scepticism can be a legitimate intellectual position, and that it accordingly follows that this kind of mental geography can yield justified conclusions. Once again, then, Hume seems to be offering his readers an assurance that he and they share a common outlook. Very few of Hume's readers would have been sympathetic to radical epistemological scepticism when they began working their way through the *Enquiry*. They might well have been pleased to find Hume apparently confirming that, whatever they might have heard about him from hostile critics, he too has no inclination to embrace such scepticism. When we look more carefully, however, it emerges that the only kind of scepticism that Hume is definitely repudiating is one that would paralyse all action and intellectual speculation. This leaves open the possibility that he is actually prepared to endorse a form of scepticism which maintains that knowledge and rationally justified belief are unattainable, but denies that these are required as a basis for action and intellectual reflection. Such a position would be an extremely virulent form of global scepticism, but it would not be incompatible with the way Hume chooses to present himself in this particular section of the *Enquiry*. And once again there would be substantial tactical advantages in preparing the basis for a defence of an unpopular or initially counter-intuitive position by persuading one's readers that these preparations were actually intended to form part of an attack on some common enemy.

Finally, we should note the way in which Hume chooses to emphasize advantages to abstract philosophy that do not rely on its capacity to uncover knowledge or rationally defensible beliefs. Natural human curiosity can be satisfied by subjectively convincing beliefs even if one has no inclination to hold that these beliefs are rationally warranted. Similarly a spirit of accuracy in non-philosophical reasonings can be promoted by attempts at abstract philosophy even if these attempts do not generate any conclusions that are immune to sceptical attack, as long as the search for such conclusions is itself intrinsically satisfying. Moreover, the destruction of the philosophical foundations of popular religion can, from Hume's perspective, be just as easily achieved by a sceptical mode of thinking as by a system of philosophy that is capable of establishing some true and warranted system of metaphysics. Hume, as we have seen, views superstition and popular religion as gaining strength from the intellectual confusion generated by the metaphysical systems invoked by their defenders. Now one way of removing that distracting influence would undoubtedly be to construct a rival and better-supported set of metaphysical doctrines. However, this outcome could also be achieved simply by the destruction of unwarranted metaphysical doctrines. In the final section of the *Enquiry*, Hume will defend at length the view that even if reflection on sceptical arguments is relatively powerless against common-sense beliefs rooted in observation and experiment, it can readily undermine the speculative systems of philosophers who rely on speculative a priori reasoning.

Questions
1. Does Hume give us an exhaustive enumeration of the sound motives for engaging in abstract philosophy as well as easy moral reflection?
2. Why is it so important to Hume that philosophy should be accessible to a general educated readership and not just a small group of

specialized scholars? Does philosophy exercise today the broad cultural influence that Hume viewed as desirable?

3. If philosophy were genuinely to be incapable of generating rationally justified beliefs, would that mean that philosophical reflection would be pointless?

2. OF THE ORIGIN OF IDEAS

a. Force and vivacity

At the start of the second section of the *Enquiry*, Hume draws our attention to the distinction between thought and the phenomena of sensation and sensory experience. According to Hume, everyone will readily admit the great difference between, for example, feeling the pain of excessive heat and remembering that heat or anticipating it by means of the imagination. Similarly, we are all familiar with the distinction between actually feeling angry and merely thinking about that emotion.

How, though, does this distinction manifest itself to us? If it is a distinction we draw with the kind of confidence envisaged by Hume, it might be expected that we should encounter no problem in specifying the basis on which we sort thoughts from sensations. Hume's own attempt at identifying this basis appeals to a difference in what he calls 'force and vivacity'. According to him, the products of the faculties of memory and the imagination lack the force and vivacity possessed by sensations and sensory experiences.

> These faculties may mimic or copy the perceptions of the senses; but they never can entirely reach the force and vivacity of the original sentiment. The utmost we say of them, even when they operate with greatest vigour, is, that they represent their object in so lively a manner that we could *almost* say we feel or see it. (2.1 / 17)

Hume then puts forward a technical vocabulary that we can use to talk in a philosophically precise way about these phenomena. Both sensation and thought are categorized as involving us in having perceptions. However, perceptions are to be treated as falling into one of two distinct classes or species, namely thoughts or ideas, and impressions. Sense experience and sensation involve being conscious of impressions, while thought is presented as a matter of being conscious of ideas. And in accordance with his view that sense experience and sensation are distinguished from thought by variations in force and vivacity, Hume says that ideas are the less forcible and lively perceptions, while the meaning of the term 'impression' is such that this covers 'all our more lively perceptions, when we hear, or see, or feel, or love, or hate, or desire, or will' (2.3 / 18).

A pressing problem with this account is how we are supposed to interpret this talk of forcefulness and vivacity. Hume himself does not offer much in the way of explanation. So it appears that he believes that the ordinary usage of 'force' and 'vivacity' will, in conjunction with our intimate acquaintanceship with thoughts, sensations, and sense experiences readily identify for us the characteristic he has in mind as the criterion on which we supposedly base our decisions about whether we are faced by an idea or an impression. However, it is often suggested (see, for example, Stroud 1977: 28–9 and Bennett 1971: 222–5) that if we take Hume's words in a fairly literal sense, his proposed criterion seems wholly implausible.

Bennett and Stroud interpret Hume as using the terms 'force' and 'vivacity' as referring to intrinsic qualities of perceptions that are analogous to the clarity and brightness of a photographic image. Just as we do not need to be aware of the causal antecedents of a photograph in order to tell whether it constitutes a clear and bright image, we do not need to know the origins of a perception in order to tell, on the basis of introspection, whether it is a forceful and lively perception. Similarly, we can determine, on this construal of Hume's position, whether a perception is forceful and lively without taking its causal consequences into account.

With this interpretation in place of how Hume wishes us to understand 'force' and 'vivacity', it is not difficult to present Hume as facing an intractable problem. Consider a case where you cast a quick glance at the items lying on top of your desk. One of those items happens to be your favourite Giuliano Mazzuoli pen. Although you pay no particular attention to it at the time, it is nevertheless something you see; and it follows that Hume would say that you have an impression of a pen. Later that day, however, you are trying to describe that pen to a friend, and you accordingly bring a very clear recollection of the pen before your mind as you attempt to explain what makes it such an aesthetically pleasing design. Here you are thinking of the pen rather than perceiving it. So Hume is officially committed to saying that you have an idea of the pen. As impressions are supposed to be more forceful and lively than mere ideas, he is also committed to saying that when you glanced at your desk the perception of the pen vouchsafed to you at that point was more forceful and lively than the perception that subsequently found a place in your thoughts. Unfortunately, if forcefulness and vivacity are understood as intrinsic properties analogous to the perceptible distinctness and brightness of an image, then it would seem that one's recollection of the pen impinges more forcibly upon one's consciousness. Yet if this point is conceded, this seems tantamount to accepting that Hume is actually implicitly committed to classifying the initial perception of the pen as an idea, and hence a mere thought, while the subsequent thought of the pen would, quite absurdly, now emerge as the impression and hence an example of a sense experience.

Fortunately, however, it is not essential to adopt the interpretation of 'force' and 'vivacity' suggested by Stroud and Bennett. If we follow Stephen Everson in treating a perception's force and vivacity as residing in its effects on our behaviour, we can give Hume a much more defensible account of the distinction between an impression and an idea. Everson makes the point that the most natural way of understanding the concepts of force and vivacity is to interpret them as causal concepts (1995: 15). Moreover, this is certainly the way Hume wishes these concepts to be understood later in the *Enquiry*. At the beginning of Section 7, Hume states:

> There are no ideas, which occur in metaphysics, more obscure and uncertain, than those of *power*, *force*, *energy*, or *necessary connexion*, of which it is every moment necessary for us to treat in all our disquisitions. (7.3 / 61–2)

And elsewhere in that section, Hume repeatedly treats the terms 'power', 'force', and 'energy' as straightforward synonyms. Thus Hume speaks, for example, of our control over our ideas as giving us 'no real idea of force or energy' (7.16 / 67); and he also claims that when we are contemplating a single example of the interaction between two bodies of a type that we have not previously encountered, we are unable 'to comprehend any force or power, by which the cause operates, or any connexion between it and its supposed effect' (7.26 / 73–4).

Once we begin to think of force and vivacity in terms of the effects that a perception with those qualities brings about, using these qualities to distinguish ideas from impressions suddenly looks much more plausible. As Hume points out himself, 'A man, in a fit of anger, is actuated in a very different manner from one who only thinks of that emotion' (2.2 / 17). In this case, then, the difference between having a particular sentiment and merely thinking about that sentiment is explained in terms of the fact that someone who is actually experiencing anger rather than simply thinking about anger has a disposition to act and think in a different way. Although this is an illustration of the difference between a sentiment and a thought, it seems fairly clear that Everson is right to hold that such an account can readily be generalized to cover the difference between all impressions and all ideas. Thus Everson maintains that the difference, for example, between perceiving that a packet of cigarettes is within reach and simply entertaining the idea of there being a packet of cigarettes to hand is a matter of the behavioural dispositions involved. Any specific actions that might ensue may depend on the agent's other beliefs and desires; nevertheless, the contribution made to a holistic explanation of the agent's behaviour by an impression of a packet of cigarettes is substantially different from the contribution made by ascribing to him a bare idea of such a packet.

> I can think about there being a packet of cigarettes in front of me and still continue to sit suffering from the increasingly unpleasant withdrawal symptoms. When I feel (perceive) that there is a packet in front of me, I will reach out to pluck a cigarette. I will indeed be 'actuated in a very different manner' from that which I would be were I only entertaining the thought. (Everson 1995: 17)

This latter interpretation of Hume's appeals to the concepts of force and vivacity can be viewed in very general terms as ascribing them functional content. A perception possesses force and vivacity only if it is capable of initiating behaviour directed towards the manipulation of the agent's environment. The intrinsic qualities of a perception fail, then, to determine whether it qualifies as an impression or as nothing more than an idea. Unless a perception of x has the effect of changing the agent's behavioural dispositions in a way that constitutes an intelligible reaction to an awareness of the presence of x, then it does not possess the force and vivacity to constitute an impression.

b. The Copy Principle

Hume's next topic in this section is the relationship between ideas and impressions. We have just been told that our ideas are characteristically less forceful than our impressions, but the question of the scope of our ideas has not yet been addressed. Hume claims that when we first consider this issue, we are likely to jump to the conclusion that there are no substantial restraints on the range of ideas we can form.

> Nothing, at first view, may seem more unbounded than the thought of man, which not only escapes all human power and authority, but is not even restrained within the limits of nature and reality. To form monsters, and join incongruous shapes and appearances, costs the imagination no more trouble than to conceive the most natural and familiar objects. (2.4 / 18)

According to Hume, however, this initial conclusion is deeply misleading. One constraint he identifies is that anything that 'implies an absolute contradiction' lies beyond the power of human thought (2.4 / 18). However, Hume is actually more interested in another constraint on the scope of our ideas. He claims that when we look carefully at the creative powers of the mind, we see that all the ideas we actually form appear to be derived from materials supplied to us by the senses and our feelings. Although we can, as Hume notes, form an idea of a golden mountain without having any previous experience of such a mountain, this ability amounts to no more than our ability to put together simpler ideas that are derived from experience. In this particular case, it is likely that we have previously seen mountains and samples of the metal gold. And, if we have never actually seen a mountain, then an alternative source of our idea of a mountain would be our acquaintanceship with such things as hills and knolls. The idea arising from encountering these lesser objects would, when combined with our idea of vast size, give us the idea of a mountain, and then we would once again be free to compound that with our idea of gold to form the idea of a golden mountain. Similarly, Hume holds that our capacity to form the idea of a virtuous horse stems from our ability to unite the idea of virtue, which we derive from our acquaintanceship with our own sentiments, with the figure and shape of a familiar animal.

The upshot is that Hume feels emboldened at this point to put forward the hypothesis that all that thought can really do is mix and compound constituent materials that ultimately derive without exception from sense perception and our inner feelings. Transposed into what Hume terms 'philosophical language', this becomes the hypothesis that 'all our ideas or more feeble perceptions are copies of our impressions or more lively ones' (2.5 / 19). This has come to be called Hume's 'Copy Principle'.

Hume supports this hypothesis with two arguments. The first is based on a challenge. According to Hume, when we put this hypothesis to the test, we find that we are always successful in uncovering a source in experience for even our most complicated or esoteric ideas. Thus he claims, by way of example, that the idea of God comes into being as a result of 'reflecting on the operations of our own mind, and augmenting, without limit, those qualities of goodness and wisdom' (2.6 / 19). The challenge, then, to anyone who denies the universal truth of this hypothesis is to produce an example of an idea that cannot be traced back to a preceding impression or set of impressions. And if such examples cannot be found, then we have persuasive grounds for concluding that the hypothesis is correct.

Hume's second argument initially looks as though it is in danger of presupposing the truth of the position that it is being used to defend. Hume argues that we invariably find that when a defect in a person's sensory organs deprives him of a particular category of impressions, he also lacks the corresponding ideas. But if the defect in the sensory organs can be remedied, then he speedily comes to possess the formerly missing ideas.

> A blind man can form no notion of colours; a deaf man of sounds. Restore either of them that sense, in which he is deficient; by opening this new inlet for his sensations, you also open an inlet for the ideas; and he finds no difficulty in conceiving these objects. (2.7 / 15)

The problem with this line of thought is that it immediately raises the question of how we are supposed to assure ourselves that the missing ideas picked out by Hume are genuinely absent in cases of sensory impairment. If possessing an idea of redness is simply a matter of being able to bring before the mind a simulacrum of an impression of redness, why should we suppose that this is something that a blind person cannot do? Asking him whether he has such an idea would get us nowhere. He might well have no idea what sense we attach to the word 'redness' even if his mind were fully stocked with mental objects that qualitatively resemble impressions of redness.

Instead of concluding, however, that this is a worthless argument, it might be advisable for us to question the appropriateness of interpreting Humean ideas as nothing more than ghostly psychic replicas of inner and outer impressions. Hume is certainly interested in giving an account of the phenomenology of conscious thought, and sensory imagery can plausibly be given a prominent role in such an account. However, Hume is also interested in arriving at an understanding of the connection between mental occurrences and action. Thus there seems to be a strong case for enriching our conception of Humean ideas and impressions. Such perceptions may indeed be mental entities or events with certain introspectible qualitative characteristics; but, as we have seen, it is plausible to suppose that Hume holds a functional account of what it is to be an impression or an idea, and of what distinguishes the two. We can think of this role in terms of recognitional capacities and behavioural dispositions. Thus a person would count as having an impression of a tiger if he has a perception that leads to his reacting as if there is a tiger in front of him. An idea of a tiger, however, would ground his capacity to recognize a tiger and to distinguish tigers from other things in one's environment. The impression, in other words, tends to activate a disposition to run and scream, whereas the idea is a perception that does not initiate action of that kind. If this is Hume's view, then possession of an idea of redness would require the person possessing that idea to have a range of practical abilities that could not be manifested by someone who lacked both that idea and the corresponding impression, and it is the absence of these abilities that we can observe in the man who has always been blind. Such a man cannot distinguish red billiard balls from white ones, and he is also unable to respond appropriately to the possession of such a discriminatory capacity by other people. The absence of these abilities does not guarantee anything about the qualitative character of any inner experiences he may happen to have, but it does entail that none of those experiences can amount to a case of his possessing an idea of redness.

c. The missing shade of blue
Somewhat surprisingly, Hume's own response to these arguments supporting the existence of a close connection between the ideas a

person can possess and his preceding impressions is to describe a way in which an idea might potentially come into existence without being copied from such correspondent impressions. Hume asserts that ideas of different shades of the same colour are distinct ideas that are not compounded from aspects of other ideas. Thus he is denying, for example, that the idea of scarlet is a compound idea constructed from the idea of redness and the idea of brightness. In the light of this understanding of our ideas of shades of colour, he then invites us to consider a person who is acquainted with a comprehensive range of colours except for one particular shade of blue.

> Let all the different shades of that colour, except that single one, be placed before him, descending gradually from the deepest to the lightest; it is plain that he will perceive a blank, where that shade is wanting, and will be sensible, that there is a greater distance in that place between the contiguous colours than in any other. Now I ask, whether it be possible for him, from his own imagination, to supply this deficiency, and raise up to himself the idea of that particular shade, though it had never been conveyed to him by his senses? I believe there are few but will be of the opinion that he can. (2.8 / 21)

Hume cheerfully agrees with this common judgement and describes the foregoing line of reasoning as constituting a 'proof' that his hypothesis concerning the origin of ideas admits of some exceptions. However, he also says that this is so singular and restricted a phenomenon that 'it is scarcely worth our observing, and does not merit, that for it alone we should alter our general maxim' (2.8 / 21). Now it might be suggested at this point that as Hume has just admitted that this general maxim is false, there could scarcely be better grounds for revising it. A charitable reading of Hume, though, would presumably treat his lack of concern over this counter-example as simply confirming that he is treating this maxim as a contingent generalization that has a plausible claim to be considered as applicable to the overwhelming majority of our ideas. If the maxim is violated only in an isolated handful of cases, we can still use it as an effective way of deciding whether someone genuinely has an idea of x. After all, a handful of exceptional free-divers can hold their breath underwater for many minutes. This does not mean, however, that it would be irresponsible for us to conclude that someone who has been submerged for 8 minutes without the aid of artificial breathing apparatus is most unlikely to still be alive. Similarly, if ideas are almost invariably derived from correspondent impressions, then it is plausible to hold of any particular idea that it is most unlikely to exist if no correspondent impression exists even if we accept that this is not impossible.

Significantly, this is the attitude Hume himself proceeds to adopt. He claims that judicious appeals to this simple and easily understood generalization about the origins of ideas will assist us to 'render every dispute equally intelligible, and banish all that jargon, which has so long taken possession of metaphysical reasonings, and drawn disgrace upon them' (2.9 / 21). Hume envisages this happening in two ways. First, if an idea is obscure and grasped only vaguely, then finding the preceding impression from which the idea is derived gives us a clearer object of investigation. As these impressions are strong and vivid, it is much easier to discern the boundaries between them and determine their true content. Second, we can use this generalization as a guide when we are confronted by a word or term that we suspect might lack a clear sense. Hume holds that repeated employment of a word can lull us into thinking that it has a determinate idea attached to it even if it actually lacks a distinct meaning. So he recommends that we should proceed as follows:

> When we entertain, therefore, any suspicion, that a philosophical term is employed without any meaning or idea (as is but too frequent), we need but enquire, *from what impression is that supposed idea derived*? And if it be impossible to assign any, this will serve to confirm our suspicion. (2.9 / 22)

Questions
1. According to Hume the imagination can copy the perceptions of the senses but the results lack the force of the originals except in a mind disordered by madness or disease. How, then, should we classify the phenomena that we seem to encounter in dreams? Are they ideas or impressions?
2. Why does Hume show no interest in distinguishing impressions from ideas in terms of their causal origins?
3. Does Hume have an excessively imagistic understanding of ideas? Even allowing for the point that he allocates ideas an important functional role, is he still guilty of misrepresenting the difference

between someone who is thinking about something and an entity that lacks an inner mental life?

3. OF THE ASSOCIATION OF IDEAS

In the 1777 posthumous edition of the *Enquiry*, this section has the distinction of being the shortest of the entire work. And it is not a particularly long section even in the preceding editions published while Hume was alive. Nevertheless, there are compelling grounds for supposing that it introduces one of the key themes of the book.

Hume's topic here is the nature of the connections between the various ideas that manifest themselves when we engage in mental reflection or go searching through our memories. Hume claims that it is obvious that in these situations our ideas do not simply emerge in a random manner. Instead, each idea that comes before the mind partially determines what idea or ideas will succeed it: 'in their appearance to the memory or imagination, they introduce each other with a certain degree of method and regularity' (3.1 / 23).

Hume's illustrations of this point draw on a diverse range of phenomena. He says that when we are thinking intently about a topic or discussing it seriously, any irrelevant idea that intrudes upon our chain of thought immediately attracts attention and is automatically rejected. He also maintains that even our most relaxed and unfocused mental meanderings still manifest the influence of some underlying unifying principles.

> And even in our wildest and most wandering reveries, nay in our very dreams, we shall find, if we reflect, that the imagination ran not altogether at adventures, but that there was still a connexion upheld among the different ideas, which succeeded each other. (3.1 / 23)

Similarly, Hume claims that these principles can be seen at work in the way that different languages that have not mutually influenced each other tend to contain words that express the same complex sets of ideas. In Hume's judgement, this is not a matter of mere chance: there must be some force at work that applies universally across cultures and disposes human beings to regard roughly the same simple ideas as sufficiently connected to be worth subsuming under a unifying linguistic term.

Hume goes on to claim that although the existence of connections between different ideas is entirely obvious, no one has yet attempted to give a complete list of all the principles of association at work here. He accordingly takes it upon himself to remedy this deficiency.

> To me, there appear to be only three principles of connexion among ideas, namely, *Resemblance*, *Contiguity* in time or place, and *Cause* or *Effect*. (3.2 / 24)

Although Hume does go to the trouble of giving a few examples of the alleged influence of these principles, he professes to be confident that the fact that they do have some role in connecting ideas together will be readily admitted by almost everyone. Much more controversy, he suspects, will be aroused by his claim that these are the only principles of association between ideas. Characteristically, he argues that the only way of settling such a dispute is to conduct a determined quest for other principles of association in cases where ideas are linked together. If we do this carefully and industriously, then our failure to find any alternative principles will ultimately constitute compelling grounds for concluding 'that the enumeration, which we form from the whole, is compleat and entire' (3.3 / 24).

This marks the end of the section in the 1777 edition of the *Enquiry*. However, all the editions published while Hume was alive contained some additional pages of material discussing the influence exerted by these three principles of association on literary works. Hume maintains that a narrative that is tightly bound together by these particular principles tends to strike us as constituting a stronger piece of writing than one where the connections are not as tight. In particular, Hume holds that if events or characters are introduced that are only loosely connected with the rest of the narration, the author makes it very difficult for the reader to sustain a high level of concern for the author's characters and their fate. An author who injudiciously makes this mistake finds that he inevitably 'loses that communication of emotions, by which alone he can interest the heart, and raise the passions to their proper height and period' (3.18).

Although the 1777 edition of the *Enquiry* was brought out after Hume's death, it is nevertheless based on Hume's own revisions to the text. Thus it is often suggested that the drastic cuts to this section in that edition reflect a waning of Hume's interest in associationist psychology. However, Buckle (2001: 142) has persuasively argued that if we look at the overall intellectual context in which Hume is working, it is at least as plausible to hold that these cuts were a product of the fact that after the publication in 1749 of Hartley's *Observations on Man*, such an approach to explaining the operations of the human mind was becoming increasingly common and almost banal. Instead of labouring points that more and more people would have been already inclined to accept, Hume could simply move on to putting his associationism to work in distinctively philosophical contexts.

Significantly, the very next section of the *Enquiry* does indeed see Hume invoking his principles of association to explain how causal reasoning manages to generate belief about unobserved matters of fact. Now it might initially be thought that such an explanation would be entirely superfluous. If causal reasoning is a rational mode of inference, why would we need any further account of why we have confidence in the results of such reasoning? However, as we will shortly see, Hume's treatment of causal reasoning is not calculated to reassure us about its rational credentials. Thus there is room for an explanation of how causal reasoning shapes our beliefs that does not presuppose that this mode of reasoning yields rationally justi- fied conclusions. And Hume's three associationist principles seem ideally suited to that role.

As said, Hume holds that there are no other principles of associ- ation operating amongst our ideas. However, it is also important to note that these three principles seem to be invoked not just as a com- plete enumeration of the principles of association, but also as a com- plete specification of all the connecting principles between our ideas. Thus Section 3 opens by referring in general terms to 'a principle of connexion between the different thoughts or ideas of the mind' (3.1 / 23), and when Hume lists his associative principles, he says there appear to be 'only three principles of connexion between ideas' (3.2 / 24). Moreover, the concluding words of this section in all the edi- tions prior to 1777 seem to make it even more clear that Hume holds that the associative principles he picks out are the only connecting principles operating on ideas within the human mind.

> It is sufficient, at present, to have established this conclusion, that the three connecting principles of all ideas are the relations of *Resemblance*, *Contiguity*, and *Causation*. (3.18)

Once we begin thinking of this list as intended to be an exhaustive list of the psychological connections between ideas, it becomes apparent that it contains one striking omission. Nowhere in this section of the *Enquiry* does Hume suggest that one idea can be connected to another by means of a rational insight into what other distinct objects would have to exist if the content of some particular idea were to be instantiated in the world. What we have in his list of three associative principles are three mechanical principles that bring about their effects without being directed or guided by any form of intelligent understanding of the world. If there is any form of rationality or reasonableness linked with these principles, it is something that emerges or evolves from their operation and not something that explains the conclusions to which they lead us. The operation of such principles is accordingly not something that would be disrupted by any worries that might arise about the inability of a particular kind of reasoning to *justify* its conclusions. So if causal reasoning, for example, is deeply rooted in our associative proclivities, we can expect it to continue to dominate our thinking even if we were to find that we had lost confidence in the rational credentials of that mode of inference.

Questions

1. How successful is this section of the *Enquiry* in preparing the way for us to accept that appeals to a special faculty of rational insight are not needed to explain the origin of our beliefs about matters of fact?

2. Is there any realistic possibility that mental regularities at the introspective level can exist without being mere symptoms of some deeper set of processes taking place in either a mental substance or a physical brain?

4. SCEPTICAL DOUBTS CONCERNING THE OPERATIONS OF THE UNDERSTANDING

a. Relations of ideas and matters of fact

Hume opens this section of the *Enquiry* with what purports to be an exhaustive characterization of the different matters of inquiry that can come before the human mind. According to Hume, such topics fall into one of two mutually exclusive categories: 'to wit, *Relations of Ideas* and *Matters of Fact*' (4.1 / 25).

The category of relations of ideas covers all true propositions that cannot be denied without self-contradiction, and all false propositions that do imply a contradiction. Moreover, Hume seems to be provisionally content to accept that the truth or falsity of propositions concerning relations of ideas can be intuitively or demonstratively certain. Although Hume will exhibit greater epistemological caution in the concluding section of the *Enquiry*, he implies in the section that we are currently considering both that a contradiction is something that can sometimes be identified with complete certainty by the human mind, and that a proposition that is self-contradictory or implies a contradiction cannot be anything other than false. Similarly, a proposition that is the negation of a proposition that is self-contradictory or implies a contradiction is presented by Hume as one that cannot be anything other than true.

Hume specifically identifies the 'sciences of Geometry, Algebra, and Arithmetic' as concerning themselves with such intuitive or demonstrative certainties (4.1 / 25); and although he does not explicitly mention deductive logic, it seems clear that it too could appropriately be included in this list of a priori intellectual disciplines. When our object of inquiry is a proposition describing a relation between ideas, the truth is supposedly discoverable:

> By the mere operation of thought without dependence on what is any where existent in the universe. Though there never were a circle or triangle in nature, the truths, demonstrated by EUCLID, would for ever retain their certainty and evidence. (4.1 / 25)

However, propositions about matters of fact are presented by Hume as requiring a very different form of supporting evidence. When we are not reflecting on a relation between ideas, any proposition we may form can be paired with an equally intelligible contrary claim. This remains the case even when we have compelling grounds for supposing that this contrary claim is, in fact, false.

> The contrary of every matter of fact is still possible; because it can never imply a contradiction, and is conceived by the mind with the same facility and distinctness, as if ever so conformable to reality. *That the sun will not rise to-morrow* is no less intelligible a proposition, and implies no more contradiction, than the affirmation, *that it will rise*. (4.2 / 25–6)

This means that if we wish to arrive at true beliefs about objects existing in the real world as opposed to beliefs about internal relations between our ideas, we cannot make use of demonstrative methods or grasp the truth of propositions about such matters through direct and intuitive awareness of their self-evidence. From Hume's point of view, these latter techniques can only be employed when we are concerned with propositions that lack intelligible contraries. So if we do regularly find ourselves with true beliefs about objects in the real world and their properties, this success needs to be explained in some radically different manner.

An appeal to the present testimony of the external senses and our sentiments offers an explanation of how we arrive at credible beliefs about many matters of fact in our immediate environment. Similarly, some beliefs about past matters of fact can be explained in terms of the operation of the memory. However, we have innumerable settled beliefs about matters of fact that do not fall into either of those two categories. Hume is accordingly concerned to discover how these beliefs arise and whether they arise in a way that allows them to conform to how things really stand.

b. Causal reasoning

According to Hume, the only form of reasoning that is even potentially capable of informing us of the existence of objects and powers that are not directly revealed to us by the senses and our memory is causal reasoning. When we move from some present fact to a conclusion about something that we have not observed, the crucial connection between them is always a causal one.

> The hearing of an articulate voice and rational discourse in the dark assures us of the presence of some person: Why? Because these are the effects of the human make and fabric, and closely connected with it. If we anatomise all the other reasonings of this nature, we shall find, that they are founded on the relation of cause and effect, and that this relation is either near or remote, direct or collateral. (4.4 / 27)

Causal reasoning thus emerges as playing an absolutely crucial role in sustaining the beliefs by which we act and live. Without such reasoning, our stock of beliefs about matters of fact would be massively impoverished. However, there is also an issue of justification to be considered. Hume implies that if we are not rationally justified in placing our confidence in the conclusions reached by orthodox causal reasoning, then none of our beliefs about the future existence of objects would be justified. Our rationally justified beliefs about past objects and their properties would, at best, be confined to our memories of what we had personally observed, and we would also be precluded from having any rationally justified beliefs about the current existence of dispositional properties or objects that lie beyond the range of our senses. Indeed, even our ability to justify giving our assent to a straightforward claim such as: 'That object I can see over there is a pen' would, on Hume's view, be undermined. After all, how could we be rationally justified in thinking that the object in question *is* a pen if we are not rationally justified in believing anything about the way it will behave in the future?

Hume's position here seems entirely plausible, but it leaves us confronting an obvious question. Under what circumstances, if any, are we entitled to infer that some unobserved event *B* will happen (or has happened) because some other event falling under our observation, *A*, can legitimately be thought of as *B*'s proximate or remote cause?

Hume's first step towards answering that question is to argue that knowledge of the existence of such a causal relationship is never attained by purely a priori reasoning, but that it always requires us to have experience of correlations between different kinds of events or objects. Hume's initial defence of this claim is provided by a thought experiment in which he invites us to consider the situation confronting someone who is attempting to predict the powers of an object that is entirely new to him.

> Let an object be presented to a man of ever so strong natural reason and abilities; if that object be entirely new to him, he will not be able, by the most accurate examination of its sensible qualities, to discover any of its causes or effects. ADAM, though his rational faculties be supposed, at the very first, entirely perfect, could not have inferred from the fluidity and transparency of water, that it would suffocate him, or from the light and warmth of fire, that it would consume him. (4.6 / 27)

Hume holds that when we are explicitly reflecting on objects that we remember to have once been wholly unfamiliar to us, we will readily concede that causal relations can only be discovered with the assistance of experience. This concession is forced from us by our recollection 'of the utter inability, which we then lay under, of foretelling, what would arise from them' (4.7 / 28). And he diagnoses any reluctance we might have to accept that prior experience is *always* required: our sheer familiarity with certain kinds of objects, and our inability to bring clearly to mind the way in which we actually came to acquire beliefs about their powers and properties, leads to us concluding that experience does not have to play such a role. The habit of inferring certain consequences from the presence of such objects is so deeply ingrained in us that we fall into the confusion of supposing that we have some non-experiential insight into their powers, even though this habit is actually no more than the product of a process of psychological conditioning brought about by our previous experiences.

> Such is the influence of custom, that, where it is strongest, it not only covers our natural ignorance, but even conceals itself, and seems not to take place, merely because it is found in the highest degree. (4.8 / 28–9)

Just in case we are not convinced by the foregoing considerations, Hume attempts to reinforce his position by asking us to consider how we could determine an object's effects without consulting previous experience. According to Hume, any beliefs that might arise in this situation about an object's effects would be wholly arbitrary and presumptuous. Any cause and its effect are logically quite distinct, and this means that from a purely a priori point of view there is nothing in the one to suggest the idea of the other. In advance of experience, any postulated pairing between causes and effects would have nothing to recommend it over and above all the other combinations that could be generated by a restless imagination. And even if we were, by sheer good fortune, lucky enough to pair some particular cause with its actual future effect, that combination would still look entirely arbitrary 'since there are always many other effects, which, to reason, must seem fully as consistent and natural' (4.11 / 30).

In summary, then, Hume holds that all our reasonings concerning matters of fact are founded on the relation of cause and effect, and he also holds that all our reasonings and conclusions in respect of causal relations are founded on experience. What, though, is the foundation of all conclusions from experience? Hume takes the view that attempting to answer this latter question is likely to be a difficult and perplexing undertaking:

> Philosophers, that give themselves airs of superior wisdom and sufficiency, have a hard task, when they encounter persons of inquisitive dispositions, who push them from every corner, to which they retreat, and who are sure at last to bring them to some dangerous dilemma. (4.14 / 32)

c. The rationality of causal inference

Despite his awareness of the difficulties facing him here, Hume makes it clear that he does regard himself as being able to offer one important negative answer to the question that he has just identified. In Hume's judgement, the conclusions we draw from our experience of the operations of cause and effect 'are *not* founded on reasoning, or any process of the understanding' (4.15 / 32).

When we make our causal inferences, we can, it seems, be legitimately represented as making an inference from the proposition that an object of a particular kind has always been attended in the past with a specific effect, to the conclusion that it will be true on future occasions that other objects that appear similar will be followed by similar effects. Hume insists that this is an inference or mental step that requires explaining because the two propositions under consideration here are plainly distinguishable in content. He tentatively expresses a willingness to accept that the one proposition 'may be justly inferred from the other', though it seems that he would prefer to restrict himself to an acknowledgement of the pervasive nature of such mental transitions: 'I know in fact, that it always is inferred' (4.16 / 34). Nevertheless, he also insists that this step is not supported by any good argument or chain of reasoning, and he endeavours to support this claim by showing that none of the modes of reasoning that might be thought to have any legitimate claim on our allegiance can give rise to such an argument.

Hume divides all our legitimate reasonings into two kinds, 'namely, demonstrative reasoning, or that concerning relations of ideas, and moral reasoning, or that concerning matter of fact and existence' (4.18 / 35). And he argues that an insuperable objection faces any attempt to invoke demonstrative arguments in the present case. Hume maintains that it is plain that we can clearly and distinctly conceive of a change in the course of nature such that 'an object, seemingly like those which we have experienced, may be attended with different or contrary effects' (4.18 / 35), and this supposition is immediately sufficient to establish that demonstrative reasoning is inapplicable here.

> Now whatever is intelligible, and can be distinctly conceived, implies no contradiction, and can never be proved false by any demonstrative argument or abstract reasoning *a priori*. (4.18 / 35)

It follows that if there is an argument in support of causal inference, it must itself be a piece of moral reasoning concerning matters of fact and existence. Yet that conclusion seems to be disastrous for the contention that a rationally acceptable argument can be found here.

At this point in the *Enquiry*, Hume has already argued that all reasoning about matters of fact and existence with even a prima facie claim to credibility is causal reasoning. Causal reasoning, though, relies upon taking our past experience of how objects of particular kinds have behaved as a guide to how similar objects will behave in the future. Hume maintains, then, that we would be using circular reasoning if we were to attempt to use moral reasoning to support the supposition that the course of nature will not change. We would be using reasoning of the very kind that is under scrutiny in respect of its trustworthiness to support the supposition that such reasoning can be trusted, and that procedure seems, as Hume points out, to be 'taking that for granted, which is the very point in question' (4.19 / 36).

Does this mean, then, that Hume has set before us an argument that forces us to accept that causal reasoning cannot generate rationally justified conclusions? Some commentators interpret Hume as having exactly this intention, but they also maintain that Hume is committed to the arbitrary and groundless claim that only deductively valid arguments can provide us with good reasons to accept their conclusions (see, for example, Stove 1973: 42–5 and Flew 1961: 87–9). On this interpretation, Hume holds that we need to be able to justify the supposition that the course of nature will remain unchanged because that is the only way of converting deductively invalid causal arguments into arguments whose premises do entail the truth of their conclusions. And his inductive scepticism is simply a product of the interaction between his mistaken view that this needs to be done and his more defensible view that the supposition in question is not one that we are capable of justifying.

It seems, however, that this particular attempt to minimize the significance of Hume's critique of causal reasoning is ultimately a failure. If we were to accept that the supposition that the course of nature will remain unchanged is not itself a rationally justified supposition, then it seems that reminding ourselves that we do not automatically reject inferences as unjustified merely because they happen to be deductively invalid would do nothing to protect causal inferences against the charge that they offer no good reason at all for accepting their conclusions as true.

Consider the situation of a scientist who admits that he has absolutely no reason to believe that the supposition that the course of nature will remain unchanged holds true of certain distinctive quantum phenomena. What would our reaction be if he went on to say that his past observations of those quantum phenomena nevertheless make it reasonable for him to believe that a specific regularity will continue to manifest itself in the future? It seems obvious that our reaction would, in fact, be one of utter bewilderment. We would find ourselves quite unable to supply any plausible interpretation of the statements in question that would not force us to conclude that at least one of these statements must be false. Moreover, this bewilderment would persist even in the face of reflection on the fact that we do not normally show any inclination to move immediately from the supposition that an inference is not deductively valid to the conclusion that it must be rationally worthless.

It appears, therefore, that our understanding of the concept of rational justification is such that even though we have no general prejudice against non-deductive inferences, we all implicitly acknowledge that it is impossible for past regularities within a given domain to provide *any* justification for claims about the future unless we are justified in endorsing the supposition that the course of nature within that domain will remain unchanged. And it seems to follow that if we agree with Hume that all our causal inferences are founded on experiential regularities, then we also have to accept that our causal inferences cannot be rationally justified unless we are rationally justified in believing, within some domain or other, that the course of nature will remain unchanged. Our open-minded willingness to consider the possibility of there being good inferences that are not deductively valid makes no difference at all to the threat posed by a potential admission that this supposition is not justified for us.

A more promising way of responding to Hume's argument would be to claim that we can be justified in accepting a supposition as true even when we are utterly unable to show, even to ourselves, that it is true. If so, Hume's critique of causal reasoning would tell us nothing about whether such reasoning *is* rationally justified, though it would tell us something very interesting about our ability to *exhibit* such reasoning as justified.

It might be claimed, moreover, that such an assessment of the upshot of Hume's discussion would better reflect Hume's own intentions. Although some of Hume's language does tend to suggest to the modern reader that he wishes to press on towards the conclusion that beliefs reached by causal reasoning are not rationally justified, it is very noticeable that his explicit argumentation concentrates on the issue of what can be said in support of our practice of making causal inferences. It is also true, as we have already noted, that Hume does say at one point that if the reader wishes to insist that such inferences are just, he would be prepared to acquiesce to that supposition (see 4.16 / 34). We should therefore take the possibility seriously that Hume's intention is only to show that we cannot explicitly formulate reasons to think that causal inferences are likely to lead to true conclusions, even though they are in fact justified.

Is it really the case, however, that the question of whether a belief is justified can be so neatly separated from the question of whether it is possible for someone to show that this belief is true or at least likely to be true? If we consider the implications of the notion of epistemic responsibility, it seems that there are, in the end, strong grounds for rejecting any attempt to deny that a positive answer to the former question requires us to be able to give a positive answer to the latter question. If a belief is justified, the thinker herself must be able to reflect on why it is likely to be true.

It is highly plausible that a person A is rationally justified in holding the belief that p only if he cannot appropriately be blamed for holding that belief. But A's blameworthiness seems to be primarily a matter of the way things appear from A's perspective. Thus it might be the case, for example, that A cannot form a mistaken belief about the content of his current conscious states. Yet if A were not aware of his infallibility, then it seems clear that this freedom from error would not suffice to protect A against the charge of proceeding irresponsibly in forming such beliefs. Moreover, A's awareness of his infallibility must amount to something more substantial than the bare belief that he cannot make a mistake. If A is to be completely free from reproach in forming his beliefs about his current states of consciousness, then he must be *justified* in believing that he is infallible. Thus the attempt to construe a rationally justified belief as one that arises from a process that is, as a matter of fact, both reliable and trusted takes us nowhere because the process of analysis cannot terminate satisfactorily without reintroducing an unanalysed appeal to the very concept we purported to be explicating.

We need, therefore, to look elsewhere for a satisfactory account of what constitutes a situation in which A cannot legitimately be reproached for holding the beliefs he does about his current states of consciousness. Ultimately it seems that A would be fully protected against such reproaches only if he were able to answer his own internal questions about the reliability of these beliefs, and he were also able to defend the belief that he is infallible in this area of inquiry against the challenges that might potentially be raised by other people. And if we generalize from this example to a conclusion about what is required for any belief to qualify as a rationally justified belief, we arrive at the conclusion that a person cannot be rationally justified in a belief unless he himself is capable of showing that this belief is true or likely to be true.

If we find ourselves believing that p but fail to conduct inquiries into that belief, then it seems clear that anybody judging our actions from the point of view of the epistemic goal of discovering the truth would have to assess us as behaving irresponsibly, unless there is some feature of our perspective on the world that entitles us to conclude that it is true that p. Suppose, for example, that A scrutinizes the contents of a room. He will, of course, form a great many beliefs about the objects in that room, and most, if not all, of these beliefs will be involuntary. However, if A is an adult human being, he can choose to undertake inquiries into the truth of the beliefs at issue here, and he would be laying himself open to a charge of epistemic irresponsibility if he fails to conduct such inquiries in all those cases where he cannot identify evidence indicating that his beliefs are true. Moreover, if A is to be completely free from reproach in not initiating and sustaining such inquiries, then it seems plain that it is not sufficient that A should have a true belief that some phenomenon constitutes the necessary evidence. A, as we have already pointed out, must be able to defend his assessment of the evidential value of this phenomenon against potential challenges and criticisms. Thus, a person is never rationally justified from a truth-seeking perspective in holding a belief unless he is able to show that belief to be true or likely to be true.

It appears, then, that there are persuasive grounds for concluding that if Hume does succeed in establishing that we can provide no good argument in support of the supposition that the course of nature will remain the same, then it is not the case that causal inferences succeed in justifying their conclusions. Of course, the fact that this negative assessment of the rationality of causal reasoning is implied by the argumentative moves Hume makes in the course of his discussion does not necessarily mean that this assessment is one that he himself takes to be correct. However, it does overturn one important consideration that might otherwise tempt us to refrain from ascribing that view to him.

Furthermore, if we take a broader perspective on the textual evidence for supposing that Hume holds back from accepting that causal reasoning cannot confer rational justification on its conclusions, it seems clear that this evidence is by no means compelling. His comment about allowing that such inferences are 'justly' made is located in a context where the emphasis is plainly on what the reader might wish to say. It is not, therefore, a good guide to Hume's own opinions. And when we look at Hume's subsequent assessment of the possible effects of his critique of causal reasoning, we find him attempting to alleviate worries that would not arise if he genuinely believed that his arguments do not challenge the rationality of this form of reasoning. In the very next section of the *Enquiry*, Hume tries to reassure us that it is psychologically impossible for arguments of the kind that he has just put forward to prevail for long over our impulse to engage in causal reasoning (see 5.2 / 41–2). Similarly, he presents this same set of arguments in the final section of the *Enquiry* as providing the sceptic with 'ample matter of triumph' (12.22 / 159), and he concentrates on explaining the psychological mechanisms that we can rely on to prevent these arguments from extinguishing our causal beliefs (see 12.23 / 159–60). As all these reassurances and explanations would be completely unnecessary if Hume were genuinely convinced that causal inferences do justify their conclusions, it seems that we can legitimately conclude that Hume's own beliefs about the rationality of causal reasoning cohere with the implications of his arguments. Not only does he provide us

with arguments that serve to undermine the view that causal reasoning yields rationally justified conclusions, but it is also the case
that he accepts that these arguments have that consequence.

Questions
1. Should we endorse Hume's contention that whatever we can
clearly conceive is logically possible?
2. Is Hume right to maintain that only causal reasoning is capable
of sustaining beliefs about matters of fact that do not fall under our
direct observation or within the scope of our memories?
3. If causal inferences are incapable of providing us with good
reasons for holding their conclusions to be true, should we try to
refrain from making such inferences?
4. Is there any plausible way of arguing that one can be rationally
justified in holding the belief that p even if one cannot show that p
is true or likely to be true? Would it make a difference if no one at all
were capable of showing that p is true or likely to be true?

5. SCEPTICAL SOLUTION OF THESE DOUBTS

a. Virtuous scepticism
The opening sentences of this section see Hume expressing worries
about the potential implications of philosophical reflection for
people's thoughts and conduct. He contends that although philosophy aims at improving our behaviour, it often has a tendency to give
added strength and force to aspects of our character that already
exercise an excessive and unbalanced influence on the way we choose
to live. He is at pains, though, to insist that not all forms of philosophical thought give rise to this danger.

> There is, however, one species of philosophy, which seems little
> liable to this inconvenience, and that because it strikes in with no
> disorderly passion of the human mind, nor can mingle itself with
> any natural affection or propensity; and that is the ACADEMIC or
> SCEPTICAL philosophy. (5.1 / 40–1)

When Hume talks about the Academics, he is referring to a
group of philosophers linked with Plato's Academy who eschewed
the dogmatic elaboration of philosophical theories in favour of a
questioning attitude based on the role allocated to Socrates in Plato's

early dialogues. These philosophers are conventionally classified together with another group of ancient philosophers, the Pyrrhonists, under the heading of sceptics. The relationship between these two groups is a very complicated one, and it is also true that the stance espoused by the Academics themselves seems to have changed considerably in the course of the history of this school (see Bailey 2002 for a detailed treatment of this topic). Moreover, it is by no means clear how well Hume is acquainted with the details of the Academic stance or, indeed, with the ways in which this differed from the outlook of the Pyrrhonean sceptics. However, Hume does give us his own summary of what he takes to be the essence of Academic scepticism:

> The ACADEMICS always talk of doubt and suspence of judgement, of danger in hasty determinations, of confining to very narrow bounds the enquiries of the understanding, and of renouncing all speculations which lie not within the limits of common life and practice. Nothing, therefore, can be more contrary than such a philosophy to the supine indolence of the mind, its rash arrogance, its lofty pretensions, and its superstitious credulity. (5.1 / 41)

As the *Enquiry* unfolds, it becomes increasingly apparent that Hume also regards the foregoing summary as an excellent characterization of both his own approach to philosophy and the chastening benefits that can arise from such an approach. Even at this stage, though, we can note that the above themes are very prominent in the preceding section of the *Enquiry*. This should not perhaps strike us as surprising, given that the title allotted to that section by Hume is 'Sceptical Doubts concerning the Operations of the Understanding'. However, it does mean that there is a special poignancy to Hume's complaint that the Academic stance, 'which, in almost every instance, must be harmless and innocent, should be the subject of so much groundless reproach and obloquy' (5.1 / 41). It seems clear that Hume is anticipating that his own views will attract similarly unfounded criticism.

The diagnosis of this phenomenon offered by Hume is that the Academic stance attracts such criticism because it opposes so many forms of intellectual folly. Hume does, however, recognize that more needs to be said to deflect the specific charge that its critique of the excessive pretensions of the human intellect might lurch catastrophically out of control and 'undermine the reasonings of common life,

and carry its doubts so far as to destroy all action, as well as speculation' (5.2 / 41). He claims that such worries are always baseless
because the natural psychological mechanisms of the human mind
are too robust to be permanently disrupted by any form of abstract
reasoning, and he develops this theme by looking at the specific
example of the critique of causal reasoning developed in the preceding section of the *Enquiry*.

b. The authority of habit and custom

Hume presents his critique of causal reasoning as leading to the conclusion that 'in all reasonings from experience, there is a step taken by
the mind, which is not supported by any argument or process of the
understanding' (5.2 / 41). However, he also maintains that even if we
are fully persuaded that this is true, there is no danger that our practice of engaging in causal inferences will be undermined. According
to Hume, if it is not argument that persuades the mind to reason
causally, then the mind must be under the control of 'some other principle of equal weight and authority; and that principle will preserve
its influence as long as human nature remains the same' (5.2 / 41–2).

What, though, is the nature of this powerful principle that exer-
cises such influence over our beliefs about the world? Hume holds
that the crucial key to its nature lies in the fact that causal inferences
occur only after we have had experience of the regular conjunction
of different kinds of events. Hume makes it clear in Section 4 that he
believes that even a person fully endowed with adult faculties of
reason and reflection would not be able to draw any inferences about
matters of fact without the assistance of experience. Moreover, even
if we suppose that this person can call upon the deliverances of the
senses to assist his inferences, Hume is adamant that no causal inferences will occur until we have experienced at least some such regular
conjunctions. And, once such experience has been acquired by
normal human beings, causal inferences will inevitably ensue even
though there is no cogent process of reasoning that validates our
willingness to engage in this form of inference.

The conclusion that Hume draws from the preceding points is that
the principle that explains our causal inferences is custom or habit.
According to Hume:

> Wherever the repetition of any particular act or operation pro-
> duces a propensity to renew the same act or operation, without

being impelled by any reasoning or process of the understanding; we always say, that this propensity is the effect of *Custom*. (5.5 / 43)

Hume is at pains to emphasize that affixing this word to the mechanism that brings about causal inferences leaves much unexplained: indeed he thinks that one of the virtues of his approach is that it opens our eyes to how far away we are from having a fully comprehensive explanation of our inferential proclivities. However, he does maintain that in linking our causal inferences in this way to custom, he has brought into the open the connection between those inferences and a psychological principle 'which is universally acknowledged, and which is well known by its effects' (5.5 / 43).

Even if we can carry our inquiries no further and we find ourselves unable to uncover any cause for the existence of this psychological disposition, Hume believes that we have made some substantial progress simply in virtue of displaying one important aspect of human psychology as the product of another psychological mechanism that already plays an important role in our explanations of human thought and behaviour. In adopting this view, Hume would have seen himself as faithfully following the methodological precepts espoused by Newton. In Newton's 'Scheme for establishing the Royal Society', for example, he sets out the following summary of the basic principles underlying experimental science or Natural Philosophy:

> Natural Philosophy consists in discovering the frame and operations of Nature, and reducing them, as far as may be, to General Rules or Laws – establishing these rules by observations and experiments, and thence deducing the causes and effects of things. (Newton 2004: ix)

Similarly, Hume has reduced one problematic mental operation – causal inference – to a particular case of a more general psychological rule, i.e. custom or habit. It is custom alone that determines us, after experience of the regular conjunction of two species of objects, to expect the one from the appearance of the other. And this has the advantage of being the only hypothesis that can adequately account for the fact that we draw 'from a thousand instances, an inference, which we are not able to draw from one instance, that is, in no respect, different from them' (5.5 / 43). According to Hume, when we are genuinely employing the faculty of reason, we only need one instance of a phenomenon to ground our conclusions: 'the conclusions, which it [reason] draws from considering one circle, are the same which it would form upon surveying all the circles in the universe' (5.5 / 43). Yet Hume is convinced that no one who has only seen one body move after impact with another in the entire course of his experience would ever have any confidence in the conclusion that every other body of a similar kind will be displaced by a like impact. Consequently Hume maintains that we can safely conclude that 'Custom, then, is the great guide of human life' (5.6 / 44). In the absence of this principle's influence, we would be devoid of belief about every matter of fact lying beyond the immediate evidence of our senses and memory. And as all voluntary action depends upon our having expectations about the future course of events, this means that without the influence of custom 'there would be an end at once of all action, as well as of the chief part of speculation' (5.6 / 45).

What now remains to be explained, however, is the nature of the difference between those cases where custom takes us to an idea of a particular kind of event, and those cases where it generates the expectation that an event of that kind will occur. It seems entirely plausible to suppose that custom and past observations can, when operating together, lead to us having the idea of one billiard ball beginning to move after being struck by another billiard ball. However, there is an obvious and important difference between entertaining or contemplating the idea of a particular kind of event and forming the confident belief that an event of that kind is about to occur.

Hume regards beliefs as enlivened ideas, ideas with a particularly high degree of force and vivacity. He maintains that the fact that we have no direct voluntary control over our beliefs suffices to establish that the difference between conceiving of it being the case that p and actually believing that p cannot be a matter of adding some special idea of existence to an idea taking p as its content.

For as the mind has authority over all its ideas, it could voluntarily annex this particular idea to any fiction, and consequently be able to believe whatever it pleases; contrary to what we find by daily experience. We can, in our conception, join the head of a man to the body of a horse; but it is not in our power to believe, that such an animal has ever really existed. (5.10 / 47–8)

He concludes that we must think of this difference as lying instead in some 'sentiment or feeling' that accompanies those ideas that constitute beliefs; one, though, that is absent in the case of mere conceptions (5.11 / 48). Such sentiments are generated in us, independently of our will, by the circumstances in which we happen to find ourselves, and we are equally incapable of eradicating them simply by willing them to be absent.

When Hume attempts to specify the nature of the relevant sentiment that transmutes ideas into beliefs, we find that he describes it in terms that parallel almost exactly his attempt in Section 2 to explicate the difference between ideas and impressions. He asserts that giving a definition of the sentiment may well be an impossible task, but he is much more confident of his ability to describe it in a potentially helpful way.

> I say then, that belief is nothing but a more vivid, lively, forcible, firm, steady conception of an object, than which the imagination alone is ever able to attain. This variety of terms, which may seem so unphilosophical, is intended only to express that act of the mind, which renders realities, or what is taken for such, more present to us than fictions, causes them to weigh more in the thought, and gives them a superior influence on the passions and imagination. (5.12 / 49)

Now it will be recalled that in our earlier discussion of Section 2, we noted that Hume also holds that impressions are ideas with a particularly high degree of force and vivacity, where force and vivacity are a matter of the influence exerted on our behaviour and other reactions. Thus there is a danger here that Hume will find himself without the resources to offer a plausible account of what we normally take to be the very different phenomena of perceiving an *x* and simply coming to acquire beliefs about an *x*, and it does have to be admitted that there are few indications in the *Enquiry* of how Hume would wish to explain this distinction. In Hume's defence, however, it should be pointed out that there are present-day authors in the field of the philosophy of mind who are prepared to treat the difference between the two situations as merely one of degree. They would argue (see, for example, Smith and Jones 1986: 115–18) that the phenomenological difference is merely a function of the difference between the rapidity with which we acquire very detailed beliefs via sense perception and the sparse content and relative unresponsiveness of the beliefs about our environment we can acquire through other means.

Hume's treatment of both beliefs and impressions as lively and forceful ideas lends itself to an attempt to present our impressions as having a strong connection with the beliefs we form about matters not lying under our direct observation. And this is certainly an approach Hume embraces enthusiastically in the case of the beliefs that arise as a result of our causal inferences. According to Hume, when we are, for example, dealing with the impression of a billiard ball being struck by another ball rather than the mere idea of such an impact, the force and vivacity of the impression carry across to the associated idea of the struck ball beginning to move. This enlivens the idea and transforms it from a mere idea to a belief, the belief that the ball will begin to move.

This result is of the utmost importance for Hume's account of human nature. Traditionally philosophers had supposed that causal inferences were mediated by the operations of deductive reasoning: in terms of the example we have just been discussing, we allegedly infer that the billiard ball will begin moving because we recognize that the idea of its remaining stationary is a priori incompatible with the idea of its being struck by another ball. And those philosophers unhappy with this explanation of our causal inferences had been inclined to suppose that these inferences arose because we were appealing to the premise that the future will be like the past. Hume, in marked contrast, offers us a radically different kind of explanation: we believe that the billiard ball will move because we see the present impact and we have acquired an associative habit as a result of seeing billiard balls and similar objects move in the past. This associative habit opens the way for a transfer of force and vivacity from our impression to the idea of the struck ball moving. Thus one might say that straightforward causal inferences are psychological transitions that occur in us as a consequence of principles that are constitutive of our nature as human beings: they are not inferences we choose to make because we recognize them as rationally justified. Given our previous experience, the belief that the billiard ball will move:

> Is the necessary result of placing the mind in such circumstances. It is an operation of the soul, when we are so situated, as unavoidable

as to feel the passion of love, when we receive benefits; or hatred, when we meet with injuries. All these operations are a species of natural instincts, which no reasoning or process of the thought and understanding is able, either to produce, or to prevent. (5.8 / 46–7)

Questions
1. Can Hume's appeal to custom or habit as a way of explaining our causal inferences successfully accommodate the fact that these inferences often lead to novel and surprising conclusions?
2. What makes a resolution of a set of doubts a 'sceptical solution'?
3. Do we need a sharper distinction between beliefs and impressions than Hume appears able to provide?

6. OF PROBABILITY

Hume has argued that causal inferences concerning matters of fact are not justified; nevertheless, it is natural for us to base our beliefs and expectations on experience. The sun has always risen, lemons have always tasted bitter, and it has always been cold at the South Pole. We therefore expect the world to carry on in this way. We do not have an a priori proof that suns, lemons and the South Pole will continue to be regular in these ways, but we are as sure as we can be that they will. Hume now introduces some terminology to mark this distinction between a priori and empirical certainty.

> LOCKE divides all arguments into demonstrative and probable. In this view, we must say, that it is only probable all men must die, or that the sun will rise tomorrow. But to conform our language more to common use, we ought to divide arguments into *demonstrations, proofs,* and *probabilities*. By *proofs* meaning such arguments from experience as leave no room for doubt or opposition. (6.1, fn. 10 / 56, fn.)

I can 'demonstrate' that if *A* is taller than *B*, and *B* is taller than *C*, then *A* is taller than *C*. Demonstrations are today more usually called a priori proofs: they are arguments that are deductively sound, the conclusions of which are necessarily true (we cannot conceive of them being false). For Hume, however, proofs are: 'arguments *from experience* as leave no room for doubt or opposition' (our emphasis). Even though we can conceive of the sun not rising tomorrow – and, therefore, it is possible that it may not – we nevertheless have a 'proof' that it will; this is because *all* my past experience supports the claim that it will continue to behave in this way. Other aspects of my experience are not so regular, yet they still lead me to have expectations about the future. Most of the oranges I have eaten have been sweet, but not all. I do not therefore have a proof that the next one will be sweet, although it is 'probable' that it will just as it is probable that rhubarb will purge and opium will stupefy (6.4 / 57–8).

> In such conclusions as are founded on an infallible experience, he expects the event with the last degree of assurance, and regards his past experience as a full *proof* of the future existence of that event. In other cases, he proceeds with more caution: He weighs the opposite experiments: He considers which side is supported by the greater number of experiments: To that side he inclines, with doubt and hesitation; and when at last he fixes his judgment, the evidence exceeds not what we properly call *probability*. (10.4 / 110–11)

Hume's terminology may strike the modern reader as a little odd. We think of proofs as infallible and certain, but this is not so for Hume: a proof can turn out to be false. However:

> One wou'd appear ridiculous, who wou'd say, that 'tis only probable that the sun will rise tomorrow, or that all men must dye: tho' 'tis plain we have no further assurance of these facts, than what experience affords us. (1739–40: 124)

It is a contingent psychological fact about people that uniform experience leaves us 'entirely free from doubt and uncertainty' (1739–40: 124); I am as sure as I can be that the next lemon I eat will be bitter, and that the sun will rise tomorrow. We should therefore say that we have proofs for such things and not that they are merely probable.

Experience, then, leads to us having various expectations about the future, some of which amount to proofs and some to 'probability judgements'. And Hume's account of belief formation explains how such varying expectations are inculcated in us by our experience. Sensory impressions of A's accompanied by sensory impressions of B's lead the mind to expect a B whenever there is an A. The larger the number of A's and B's, the stronger the belief that they will continue to occur together. Conversely, experiencing an A without a B leads to a weakened belief in the continuing concurrence of A's and B's.

> But finding a greater number of sides concur in the one event than in the other, the mind is carried more frequently to that event, and meets it oftener, in revolving the various possibilities or chances, on which the ultimate result depends. This concurrence of several views in one particular event begets immediately, by an inexplicable contrivance of nature, the sentiment of belief, and gives that event the advantage over its antagonist, which is supported by a smaller number of views. (6.3 / 57)

If x is the number of times that A and B have occurred together, and y is the number of times that they have not, then the strength of my belief in the next A occurring with a B will be a function of the ratio of x to y. Imagine that you are manipulating a photograph of a yellow banana using a photo-editing programme with '+' and '−' keys for brightness. Every time you see a yellow banana you tap the '+' key and the brightness of the photograph slightly increases; every time you see a green or black banana you tap the '−' key and the brightness slightly decreases. The strength of your belief that the next banana will be yellow is proportional to the brightness of the edited image.

> There is . . . a probability, which arises from a superiority of chances on any side; and according as this superiority encreases, and surpasses the opposite chances, the probability receives a proportionable encrease, and begets still a higher degree of belief or assent to that side, in which we discover the superiority. (6.2 / 56)

Empirical reasoning does not depend on argument, but rather, on the mechanistic, associative processes involved in the transfer of vivacity to our ideas: 'all probable reasoning is nothing but a species of sensation' (1739–40: 103).

If there is not 'a superiority of chances on any side', then we do not come to have beliefs about a particular outcome.

The mind is determin'd to the superior only with that force, which remains after subtracting the inferior. (1739–40: 138)

When we transfer the past to the future . . . every past experiment has the same weight, and . . . 'tis only a superior number of them, which can throw the balance on any side. (1739–40: 136).

Tossed coins have landed on tails as many times as they have landed on heads, and therefore no net vivacity is transferred to either the idea of a head or to the idea of a tail. Here we can imagine a photograph of a head and a programme that adjusts the sharpness according to whether the '+' and '−' keys are tapped. Every time a tail is tossed you press the '−' key and the head on the photograph becomes less distinct. Our idea of a head does not have sufficient vivacity to constitute a belief, just as the relevant features of the coin cannot be discerned on the resultant photograph.

There are some differences between Hume's account of probability and belief, and the one that is adopted today. Hume's probabilities do not lie on a scale of 0 to 1, with 1 corresponding to certainty and 0 to impossibility. We have already noted that certainty and impossibility do not apply to empirical knowledge (only to demonstrations). At the bottom of Hume's scale we have cases like that of the coin where the 'superior' is equal to the 'inferior'. Both the idea of a head and that of a tail have zero superior force or vivacity, whereas on a modern account they each have a probability of $\frac{1}{2}$. Also, the top of Hume's scale is not indexed to 1. Proofs are not certain in a demonstrative sense, and they can be of different strengths dependent on the number of 'experiments' in support of them. The more A's that occur with B's, the more vivacity that is transferred and the stronger our belief.

Hume's notion of probability is not mathematical: one that can be calculated a priori and that is indexed to certainty and impossibility. It is, instead, part of his naturalistic account of empirical belief formation. And, as we shall go on to see, it plays an important role in his accounts of liberty and necessity (Section 8) and of religious belief (Sections 10 and 11).

Questions
1. What does Hume mean when he says that 'all probable reasoning is nothing but a species of sensation'? (Hume 1739–40: 103).
2. According to Hume, are the following demonstrable, provable or probable?

(i)   Bachelors are unmarried.
(ii) Water is wet.
(iii) 2 + 2 = 4.
(iv) Night follows day.
(v)   Caffeine perks me up.
(vi) Every event has a cause.

3. How can Hume claim that it is 'probable' that my soufflé will rise in the oven, when he has argued that there is no reason to think that the future will resemble the past?

7. THE IDEA OF NECESSARY CONNECTION

Hume's account of causation is central to the *Enquiry* and to the discussion of miracles (Section 10), liberty and necessity (Section 8), and natural religion (Section 11). Further, the views that we find here and in the *Treatise* have shaped all subsequent discussion of this key metaphysical issue.

a. The idea of necessary connection

When a brick causes a window to smash, we do not just have an impression of the trajectory of the brick followed by an impression of breaking glass; we also think of the brick *causing* or *bringing about* the shattering. Given the weight and path of the brick we believe, not just that the glass will break, but that it *must*. To say that there is a causal relation between two events – e.g. between flying bricks and breaking glass – is to say that there is a 'necessary connection' between them. Section 7 investigates the origin of this idea.

> There are no ideas, which occur in metaphysics, more obscure and uncertain, than those of *power, force, energy*, or *necessary connexion* . . . We shall, therefore, endeavour, in this section, to fix, if possible, the precise meaning of these terms, and thereby remove some part of that obscurity, which is so much complained of in this species of philosophy. (7.3 / 61–2)

Rationalists such as Descartes claim that causes have an inherent 'efficacy, agency, power, force, energy . . . and productive quality' (Hume 1739–40: 157). This explains why they necessarily bring about certain effects. This power is also *intelligible*, that is, we can come to know its nature and, in doing so, we are able to reason – a priori – that a particular cause will bring about a particular effect. Causal relations are intelligible in the same way as mathematical propositions: reflection upon right-angled triangles reveals that the square of the hypotenuse is (and must be) the sum of the squares of the two other sides. Such reflection also reveals that bricks of a certain size will (and must) break panes of glass.

> It must be allowed, that, when we know a power, we know that very circumstance in the cause, by which it is enabled to produce the effect: For these are supposed to be synonimous. We must, therefore, know both the cause and effect, and the relation between them. (7.17 / 67–8)
>
> But were the power or energy of any cause discoverable by the mind, we could foresee the effect, even without experience; and might, at first, pronounce with certainty concerning it, by the mere dint of thought and reasoning. (7.7 / 63)

Hume, however, denies that we can have a priori knowledge of causation: 'To consider the matter *a priori*, any thing may produce any thing' (Hume 1739–40: 247). We must turn to empirical evidence to discover the effects of particular causes and to find the source of the idea of necessary connection.

> When any natural object or event is presented, it is impossible for us, by any sagacity or penetration, to discover, or even conjecture, without experience, what event will result from it, or to carry our foresight beyond that object. (7.27 / 75)

b. The search for the impression of necessary connection
All ideas for Hume are derived from impressions.

> It is impossible for us to *think* of any thing, which we have not antecedently *felt*, either by our external or internal senses. (7.4 / 62)
>
> Every idea is copied from some preceding impression or sentiment; and where we cannot find any impression, we may be certain that there is no idea. (7.30 / 78)

The idea of necessary connection must therefore be derived from an impression of necessary connection, from our experience of the necessary relation between causes and effects. In Part 1 of this section Hume considers three possible sources of this impression. First, our experience of observable causal relations such as when a billiard ball causes another to move; second, the causal relations of our own minds, when, for example, my desire for coffee causes me to reach for my coffee cup; and third, cases where God is (allegedly) responsible for causal action. We shall find, though, that this initial search for the impression of necessary connection is unsuccessful, and, in Part 2 of this section, that the actual origin of this idea is rather unexpected.

When I watch one billiard ball hitting another, I think that the first ball causes the second to move; I take the movement of the two balls to be necessarily connected. Watching billiards should therefore provide me with an impression of necessary connection, and thus, empirical evidence of necessity. However:

> When we look about us toward external objects, and consider the operation of causes, we are never able, in a single instance, to discover any power or necessary connexion; any quality, which binds the effect to the cause, and renders the one an infallible consequence of the other. We only find, that the one does actually, in fact, follow the other. The impulse of one billiard-ball is attended with motion in the second. This is the whole that appears to the *outward* senses . . . Consequently, there is not, in any single, particular instance of cause and effect, any thing which can suggest the idea of power or necessary connexion. (7.6 / 63)

I do not *see* the force or power of the first ball causing the second to move; observation, therefore, is not the source of my impression of necessary connection. Imagine a trick billiard table where the two balls do not actually impact: the first ball stops just short of the second, but this is nevertheless caused to move by magnets under the table and by a steel core within the ball. The first ball does not cause the second to move – their movements are not necessarily connected – yet, to an observer, this illusion is indistinguishable from the normal case in which the movements of the balls are causally related. There is nothing extra to *see* in the causal case, and therefore the necessary connection between the two balls is not observable.

If we cannot see necessity in the world, perhaps we are aware of it in the operations of our own minds. My desire for coffee causes my arm to move, and thinking of Paris causes me to form an image of the Eiffel Tower. Since these are causal relations I may be able to find an impression of necessary connection by reflecting upon these mental processes. It may be that:

> We are every moment conscious of internal power; while we feel, that, by the simple command of our will, we can move the organs of our body, or direct the faculties of our mind. An act of voli-tion produces motion in our limbs, or raises a new idea in our imagination. This influence of the will we know by consciousness. Hence we acquire the idea of power or energy . . . (7.9 / 64)

However:

> Reflect upon it [volition]. Consider it on all sides. Do you find any thing in it like this creative power, by which it raises from nothing a new idea . . . So far from being conscious of this energy in the will, it requires . . . experience . . . to convince us that such extraordinary effects do ever result from a simple act of volition. (7.20 / 69)
>
> But the means, by which this is effected; the energy, by which the will performs so extraordinary an operation; of this we are so far from being immediately conscious, that it must for ever escape our most diligent inquiry. (7.10 / 65)

Hume puts forward three arguments for why we are not aware of the causal power that our minds have over our bodies. First, if we were aware of such power we would know how it operated.

> When we know a power, we know that very circumstance in the cause, by which it is enabled to produce the effect. (7.17 / 67–8)

This, however, is something that we do not know or understand.

> Is there any principle in all nature more mysterious than the union of soul with body; by which a supposed spiritual substance acquires such an influence over a material one, that the most refined thought is able to actuate the grossest matter? (7.11 / 65)

Second, if we were aware of the causal power of our minds, then we would know why it is that we can will our fingers to move but not our liver, that is, why only some parts of the body are under our voluntary control.

> Being in that case fully acquainted with the power or force, by which it operates, we should also know, why its influence reaches precisely to such boundaries, and no farther. (7.12 / 65)

Again this is something that we do not know or understand.

Third, the movement of my arm when I reach for the coffee is the end point in a long chain of physical causes. One link in the chain involves nerve impulses triggering the contraction of a muscle in my arm. However, I am not aware of the causal influence I have over this mechanism, and therefore such action cannot be the source of my impression of necessary connection. All I *feel* – all I am aware of – is my desire for coffee, followed by the sensory impression of my arm moving.

Imagine that your nervous system has been modified by a physiologist who uses a brain scanner to detect when you have certain volitions. The neurons connecting your brain to your arm muscles have been severed, but the physiologist is able to trigger the contraction of those muscles via remote control. According to Hume, if such triggering were performed just after you willed your arm to move, then your experience of this action would be indistinguishable from that in which the usual physiological causes were operative. All you experience is *A* followed by *B* – volitions followed by actions – you do not have a sensory impression of those actions being necessarily connected to those volitions. We are not able to 'observe or conceive the tye, which binds together the motion and volition, or the energy by which the mind produces this effect' (7.26 / 74).

> We learn the influence of our will from experience alone. And experience only teaches us, how one event constantly follows another; without instructing us in the secret connexion, which binds them together, and renders them inseparable. (7.13 / 66)

Hume then uses the same three arguments to show that causal powers are not evident in our ability to bring certain ideas and thoughts before the mind. First, our power to call up ideas is 'entirely beyond our comprehension' (7.17 / 68). Second, we have more control over our ideas than we do over our sentiments and passions, but we do not know why. And third:

> Is there not . . . either in a spiritual or material substance, or both, some secret mechanism or structure of parts, upon which the effect depends, and which, being entirely unknown to us, renders the power or energy of the will equally unknown and incomprehensible? (7.19 / 68)

Hume concludes:

> Our idea of power is not copied from any sentiment or consciousness of power within ourselves. (7.15 / 67)

Occasionalists such as Melebranche argue that God is the immediate cause of both the movement of physical bodies and the operations of our mind. All causes are 'occasions' on which God intervenes. When billiards is being played it is God that causes me to hit the white ball in a certain way, and 'it is the Deity himself, they say, who, by a particular volition, moves the second ball' (7.21 / 70). Physical objects or human minds do not have causal powers; only God does: 'according to these philosophers, every thing is full of God' (7.22 / 71). Hume thinks this theory is conceived in 'fairy land' (7.24 / 72)! However, even if such a theory were persuasive, it would not help us in our search for the impression of necessary connection since we are:

> Equally ignorant of the manner or force by which a mind, even the supreme mind, operates either on itself or on body. (7.25 / 72)

Hume has argued that necessity cannot be found in observable causal relations or in the operations of our minds or the actions of God. Thus:

> There appears not, throughout all nature, any one instance of connexion, which is conceivable by us. All events seem entirely loose and separate. One event follows another; but we never can observe any tye between them. They seem *conjoined*, but never *connected*. (7.26 / 74)

The energy of the cause is . . . unintelligible . . . we only learn by experience the frequent CONJUNCTION of objects, without being ever able to comprehend any thing like CONNEXION between them. (7.21 / 69)

Let an object be presented to a man of ever so strong natural reason and abilities; if that object be entirely new to him, he will not be able, by the most accurate examination of its sensible qualities, to discover any of its causes or effects. (4.6 / 27)

In all single instances of the operation of bodies or minds, there is nothing that produces any impression, nor consequently can suggest any idea, of power or necessary connexion. (7.30 / 78)

c. The role of the imagination

We have not yet found the source of our idea of necessity. It is not something of which we have a priori knowledge, and it is not derived from a sensory impression, or from an impression gained by reflecting on the operations of the mind (either ours or God's). There is, however, one last place to look and that is in the imagination.

In Part 2 of this section Hume argues that the impression of necessary connection is produced by the imagination after we have experienced a constant conjunction between two types of event. When we first encounter fire and heat, we do not take them to be necessarily or causally connected. However, after experiencing fire and heat together a good number of times the mind is led, by habit, to expect heat whenever there is fire. This expectation cannot be justified by reason (Section 4); we just find it natural to think in this way. We saw earlier how the associative mechanisms behind such thinking lead to belief (Section 5). A further product of these habitual cognitive processes is a 'feeling of determination', a feeling that such belief and expectation are inevitable and unavoidable; I feel that I cannot help but think that the fire will be hot. This feeling is the impression of necessary connection.

Our idea, therefore, of necessity and causation arises entirely from the uniformity, observable in the operations of nature; where similar objects are constantly conjoined together, and the mind is determined by custom to infer the one from the appearance of the other. (8.5 / 82)

After a repetition of similar instances, the mind is carried by habit, upon the appearance of one event, to expect its usual attendant, and to believe, that it will exist. This connexion, therefore, which we *feel* in the mind, this customary transition of the imagination from one object to its usual attendant, is the sentiment or impression, from which we form the idea of power or necessary connection. Nothing farther is in the case. (7.28 / 75)

However, we believe that things in the world stand in causal relations to each other – that fire causes heat, and that a billiard ball causes another to move – and not just that our mind slips easily from the experience of one to the thought of its usual accompaniment. But why do we think of the world in this way? Why do we think of objects themselves as causally related? Hume's answer is that:

As we *feel* a customary connexion between the ideas, we transfer that feeling to the objects; as nothing is more usual than to apply to external bodies every internal sensation, which they occasion. (7.29, fn. 17 / 77, fn.)

In the *Treatise* Hume talks about the mind 'spreading itself' on objects in the world. We 'project' necessity on to the world: the ease with which the mind moves from *A* to *B* makes us believe that *A*'s themselves are necessarily connected to *B*'s. We are, however, mistaken. There is no empirical evidence – the only evidence that there can be for Hume – that there are necessary connections actually in the world.

When we say, therefore, that one object is connected with another, we mean only, that they have acquired a connexion in our thought . . . (7.28 / 76)

Hume's conclusions are problematic in various ways. First, it is not clear whether Hume has correctly identified the kind of thing that can constitute an *impression* of necessity. The mind may easily move from an impression of *A* to the thought of *B*, but this is simply a fluent movement, or mental operation; it is not an impression which, for Hume, is a type of perception.

Second, Hume's account of causation is 'subjectivist'. Our idea of necessity, an essential component of the idea of causation, is a product of the mechanics of the mind. A consequence of such an account would therefore seem to be that if there were no minds, then there would be no causation. There would only be certain types of objects constantly conjoined with others. Things do not have a causal effect on each other; they merely follow one another in more or less regular patterns. In the *Treatise* Hume notes the problematic nature of this claim.

> What! the efficacy of causes lie in the determination of the mind! As if causes did not operate entirely independent of the mind, and wou'd not continue their operation, even tho' there was no mind existent to contemplate them, or reason concerning them. Thought may well depend on causes for its operation, but not causes on thought. This is to reverse the order of nature, and make that secondary, which is really primary. (Hume 1739–40: 167)

Some philosophers, however, have argued that Hume does believe in objective causal connections between objects, and it is this new interpretation of Hume that we shall go on to discuss.

d. The New Hume debate: the regularity theory of causation

The traditional interpretation takes Hume to be claiming that causation consists only in constant conjunction. *A*'s are said to cause *B*'s when *A*'s are constantly conjoined with *B*'s. *A*'s do not, however, have the *power* or *force* to *produce* *B*'s. This is called the regularity theory of causation.

> This constancy forms the very essence of necessity, nor have we any other idea of it. (8.25, fn. 19 / 96, fn.)

We may project more onto the world – objective causal powers – but we are mistaken in thinking that objects actually possess such powers. There are, though, some problems with this account of causation. The first concerns Hume's two definitions of a 'cause'.

> (1) we may define a cause to be *an object, followed by another, and where all the objects, similar to the first, are followed by objects similar to the second. Or in other words, where, if the first object had not been, the second never had existed.* (7.29 / 76)

And:

(2) another definition of *cause* [is] . . . *an object followed by another, and whose appearance always conveys the thought to that other*. (7.29 / 77)

The first definition only refers to what there is in the world – regular patterns – whereas the second also refers to what happens in our minds when we experience such regularities. Hume claims that 'both these senses [of causation] are, at bottom, the same' (8.27 / 97). However, many interpreters of Hume have pointed out that this cannot be so because the two definitions do not pick out the same set of putative causes and effects. There are things that would be classified as causes according to one definition yet not according to the other. *A* is a cause of *B* according to (1), if *A*'s and *B*'s have been constantly conjoined, yet if *A*'s and *B*'s are not observed, then (2) would not class this relation as causal. *A*'s and *B*'s may be out of sight, or perhaps too small or too far away ever to be observed, and, according to (2), relations are only causal if they lead to the requisite association in an observer's mind. There are also cases that satisfy (2) but not (1). Matthew has always felt queasy after eating a meal that contains peas. Whenever he sees peas on his plate his mind is led to the thought of illness; he believes that peas cause him to be sick. According to (2), peas should therefore be seen as playing such a causal role since their 'appearance always conveys the thought to that other', that is, to illness. Matthew, however, is mistaken: peas are not constantly conjoined with illness. It is not the case that '*if the first object had not been, the second never* . . . [would have] *existed*.' Here, then, (2) is satisfied but (1) is not. These two definitions are not therefore the same.

However, Hume's position can be seen as coherent if it is noted that, for him, 'definition' does not have its modern usage. Definitions in modern analytic philosophy describe the necessary and sufficient conditions that must be satisfied in order that one correctly ascribes a particular concept. Such definitions are derived through conceptual analysis. A conceptual analysis of 'cause' would describe the properties that a cause must have (necessary conditions) and the properties that would suffice (sufficient conditions) for something to be called a cause. This cannot be Hume's aim because the contradictory conclusion would then follow that it is correct to call peas the cause of illness, according to the necessary and sufficient conditions described by (2) and also that it is not correct to do so, according to (1). Instead, Hume's definitions should be given a naturalistic interpretation: they describe in two different ways the conditions under which we come to believe in the existence of causal relations. Definition (1) states what must be present in the world for this to be so, and (2) states the cognitive mechanisms that must operate in a thinker for her to have such beliefs.

It could also be argued that actually both of Hume's definitions do classify the same set of objects as causes. First, throughout the *Enquiry* Hume is concerned with the mechanics of belief and so it is clear that he intends (1) to be read conditionally, that is, it is implicit that such regularity only defines a cause *if* that regularity were observed. Second, to avoid the problem of a thinker mistakenly taking two kinds of things to be constantly conjoined when they are not – e.g. peas and illness – thinkers should be seen as *idealized*: one should only consider thinkers who have experienced representative samples, that is, samples that include, in this case, peas that are not followed by illness. If Hume's definitions are read in this way, then they pick out the same objects as causes.

Another problem for the regularity theory of causation is that there would seem to be cases of constant conjunction that are not indicative of causal relations. First, there could be regularities that are purely accidental. It just so happens that it has rained every time Alfred has gone to the Lake District. Alfred's visits do not cause it to rain; it is just coincidental that it always does whenever he is there. A regularity theory cannot distinguish such coincidences from cases in which two kinds of events are causally related. Second, A's and B's may be constantly conjoined because they are both the product of a common cause (C). A certain disease may be the cause of, first, a skin rash and then, a little later, cold sweats. The presence of this disease is therefore constantly conjoined with both of these symptoms. It follows that this kind of skin rash is constantly conjoined with cold sweats (If C is constantly conjoined with A *and* B, then A is constantly conjoined with B). A regularity theorist would therefore have to say that cold sweats are caused by this rash. This does not seem right; it is the underlying disease that is the cause of both symptoms. I say 'seem' because the 'heroic Humean' strategy is to bite the bullet and to claim that in such cases it is correct to say that A causes B, that this rash causes cold sweats (see Mackie 1980: 198).

Such a strategy would also deny that there is a distinction between accidental and causal regularities: Alfred's visits do cause it to rain. In all cases causation is just constant conjunction.

A distinct response to such examples is to say that there is an objective difference between accidental and causal regularities, and that the relation between skin rashes and cold sweats should not be seen as causal because it lacks a property that all causal relations must possess. This property consists in the metaphysical causal powers that Hume allegedly rejects; recently, however, some have argued that Hume allows for their existence.

e. The New Hume

Everyone agrees that Hume makes at least an epistemological point: we do not have knowledge of causal powers. Reason or observation cannot provide us with insight into the metaphysical question of what lies behind the shifting patterns of our experience. On the old interpretation of Hume, this is because the answer to this question is 'Nothing': it is just a brute fact that there are regular patterns in the world. Proponents of the new interpretation of Hume, such as Strawson (1989), agree with the epistemological claim: we cannot come to know that there are causal powers through observation or a priori reasoning. Causal powers, though, do exist; it is these that explain why the world is a regular place. It is claimed that this New Humean position is more consistent with Hume's sceptical, anti-dogmatic stance. The Old Hume forwards metaphysical claims about the nature of reality: causal powers do not exist; causation is just constant conjunction. The New Hume, however, does not claim to *know* whether or not there are causal powers (although he *believes* that there are), and his agnostic *epistemological* claim should not be seen as having *metaphysical* ramifications: just because we do not have knowledge of causal powers does not entail their non-existence. Quotations are found in Hume to support this new interpretation. The following all suggest that causation does depend on certain 'secret springs' or causal powers – powers, however, that are hidden from us.

> Nature has kept us at a great distance from all her secrets, and has afforded us only the knowledge of a few superficial qualities of objects; while she conceals from us those powers and princi-ples, on which the influence of these objects entirely depends . . . [A]s to that wonderful force or power . . . of this we cannot form

the most distant conception. But notwithstanding this ignorance of natural powers and principles, we always presume, when we see like sensible qualities, that they have like secret powers. (4.16 / 32–3)

But as to the causes of these general causes, we should in vain attempt their discovery . . . These ultimate springs and principles are totally shut up from human curiosity and enquiry. (4.12 / 30)

The scenes of the universe are constantly shifting, and one object follows another in an uninterrupted succession; but the power or force, which actuates the whole machine, is entirely concealed from us, and never discovers itself in any of the sensible qualities of body. (7.8 / 63–4)

We are ignorant of those powers and forces, on which this regular course and succession of objects totally depends. (5.22 / 55)

The New Hume is a realist about causal powers – he believes that there is something in virtue of which the world is regular – but he is agnostic about their nature since that is epistemologically inaccessible to us. Hume's definitions of cause can therefore be seen as only making reference to the accessible empirical evidence and not to causes themselves.

It is impossible to give any just definition of *cause*, except what is drawn from something extraneous and foreign to it . . . both these definitions be drawn from circumstances foreign to the cause . . . (7.29 / 76)

One problem for the New Humean is that this interpretation does not seem to be consistent with Hume's idea theory of meaning or his empiricism. According to Hume, we can only have ideas concerning aspects of the world that we have experienced, and, as causal powers are 'entirely concealed from us, and never [discover themselves] in any of the sensible qualities of body' (7.8 / 63–4), then we cannot possess ideas concerning them. This entails, not just that we cannot have knowledge of causal powers, but also that we cannot think about them at all; we cannot wonder about their existence because we do not understand what such causal powers are supposed to be – we have no genuine idea of them. It is meaningless to talk of causation as anything over and above constant conjunction, that of which we do have experience.

The power or energy . . . is unknown and inconceivable. (7.15 / 67)

We have no idea of this connexion; nor even any distinct notion of what it is we desire to know, when we endeavour a conception of it. (7.29 / 77)

And as we can have no idea of any thing, which never appeared to our outward sense or inward sentiment, the necessary conclusion *seems* to be that we have no idea of connexion or power at all, and that these words are absolutely without any meaning, when employed either in philosophical reasonings, or common life. (7.26 / 74)

We know, that, in fact, heat is a constant attendant of flame; but what is the connexion between them, we have no room so much as to conjecture or imagine. (7.8 / 64)

Hume cannot therefore be interpreted as a realist about causal powers; he cannot believe in their existence if they are not 'even conceivable by the mind'. Beliefs are vivid ideas; thus, if one cannot have an idea of causal power, then one cannot believe in its existence either.

New Humeans must find a way to avoid this conclusion: it has to be shown that we can (in some sense) know what we are talking about when talking of causal powers, even though we cannot come to have knowledge of their nature. Strawson attempts to use the distinction between 'supposing' and 'conceiving' to do this. We may not be able to conceive of causal powers, but we can nevertheless suppose they exist.

The generality of mankind . . . *suppose*, that, in all these cases, they perceive the very force or energy of the cause, by which it is connected with its effect . . . (7.21 / 69; our emphasis)

We *suppose*, that there is some connexion between them; some power in the one, by which it infallibly produces the other, and operates with the greatest certainty and strongest necessity. (7.27 / 75; our emphasis)

When we conceive of something we are aware of a certain idea – an image is before the mind – and all such ideas are derived from our sensory impressions. Suppositions, however, involve 'relative ideas'. I do not know what caused my lilies to die this year; I have no idea or image of what was responsible. I can, though, still think about what caused their demise and this is because I can have a relative idea with the content, 'whatever it is that killed my lilies'. Via relative ideas we can think about things that we have not directly experienced; we can think about things even though we do not know exactly *what* they are. Thus, we can suppose that causal powers exist since we can have a relative idea of 'whatever it is that actuates the whole machine', without knowing anything further about *what* plays this role. We can therefore think about things even though we do not have the requisite non-relative ideas, those which are directly derived from our sensory impressions. If this is so, then Hume can be a realist about causal powers: he can think about them and believe that they exist.

Conversely, the Old Humean also has difficulties providing a coherent interpretation of Hume's position. It must be explained why Hume seems to refer to 'secret [causal] powers' in the quotations above, those that the New Humean takes to support the realist interpretation. The Old Humean can reply: first, that just because Hume talks of such powers, this does not entail that he believes they exist. To say that I have no knowledge of fairies is consistent with the claim that I do not believe in their existence. I use the term 'fairy' for the sake of argument, even though I do not think that it refers to anything in the world. Hume could therefore talk of 'causal powers' even though he does not believe in their existence. Second, the key to the traditional interpretation is found in two footnotes. Hume points out that:

> The word, *power*, is here used in a loose and popular sense. The more accurate explication of it would give additional evidence to this argument. (4.16, fn. 7 / 33, fn.)
>
> As to the frequent use of the words, *force, power, energy, etc.* which every where occur in common conversation, as well as in philosophy; that is no proof, that we are acquainted, in any instance, with the connecting principle between cause and effect, or can account ultimately for the production of one thing by another. These words, as commonly used, have very loose meanings annexed to them; and their ideas are very uncertain and confused. (7.29, fn. 17 / 77–8, fn.)

Reading the *Enquiry*, we could mistakenly take 'causal powers' and the like to be used in their 'loose and popular' sense, that is, as referring to the underlying metaphysical forces behind nature. This, however, is not so. Hume explains in this section – 'Section 7' – that an object has causal power or force if it is constantly conjoined with a certain effect (and if it leads the mind to think of its usual accompaniment). And a *secret* power is a regularity that is yet to be observed, the kind of regularity that science aims to uncover. Hume's talk of 'secret powers' is therefore compatible with the traditional interpretation of Hume, and with the claim that causation is nothing over and above constant conjunction. Rutherford (the first physicist to split the atom) once remarked that 'all science is either physics or stamp collecting'. On a Humean picture, however, physics is also akin to stamp collecting. Physics does not uncover the metaphysical forces that actuate the whole machine; it just describes and collates more and more precise empirical generalizations.

This debate between the traditional and the new interpretation of Hume is still very much alive. We shall take a side and throughout the rest of the book the following interpretation of Hume shall be accepted. This is an austere version of the new interpretation. Hume is not dogmatic: it is *possible* that there are causal powers. There is, however, no *reason* to believe in them; the only reasons there could be are ones that are a priori or empirical, and Hume has argued that neither of these are valid. The only kind of causation that we can come to have knowledge of is that which consists of constant conjunction. The imagination, however, leads us to have unjustified beliefs about the causal structure of the world.

> Men still entertain a strong propensity to believe, that they penetrate farther into the powers of nature, and perceive something like a necessary connexion between the cause and the effect. (8.21 / 92)

We cannot avoid this: we habitually project necessary connections onto the world. However much scepticism infuses Hume's discussion of causation, he cannot help but believe that the world contains necessity. This belief is not warranted by the evidence; it is simply foisted on us by our imagination. What, then, is causation? The only clear idea we have of causation is that it is constant conjunction.

Questions
1. If there were no sentient creatures on Earth, would the sun cause the temperature to rise?
2. While weight-training I do not just have the experience of physical effort followed by the experience of seeing my dumb-bells rise

into the air; rather, I feel myself *forcing* them into the air. Do I? And what relevance does this have to Hume's claim concerning the impression of necessary connection?

3. I do not only see the movement of billiard balls; I also see the cue tip *making* the cue ball move, and the white *setting* the red *in motion* towards the pocket; I see the billiard player *producing* the motion on the table. Do I? What would Hume say about these claims?

4. *Every* time that I sit down to read a certain novel, the telephone rings and disturbs me. Is it possible, according to Hume, to see this as coincidental? (Or must the constant conjunction here lead me to see these events as causally related?)

5. Days are constantly conjoined with nights, and the thought of night-time leads my mind to think of the forthcoming day. Days therefore cause nights. Do they?

6. If it were possible to switch the imagination off, what would our experience of the world be like? And what would we claim about the nature of causation?

8. OF LIBERTY AND NECESSITY

In Section 8 Hume turns to certain fundamental issues concerning the metaphysics and morality of human beings. He argues that free human action is necessitated, and it is only because this is so that people can be seen as morally responsible.

a. The regularity of human action

We have seen that, according to Hume, there is no reason to believe in objective causal powers. We do, however, see the world in terms of causal relations, and the causal events are those where our experience of event *A* leads us to expect the occurrence of its usual accompaniment, event *B*. We have such expectations because *A* and *B* have been constantly conjoined in the past. The necessary causal connections we see in the world are a reflection of expectations that have been inculcated in us by regularities in our experience. Hume now applies this notion of causality and necessity to human action, and he claims that the actions of people are as regular as the mechanistic behaviour of the physical world.

It is universally acknowledged, that there is a great uniformity among the actions of men, in all nations and ages, and that

human nature remains still the same, in its principles and operations. The same motives always produce the same actions: The
same events follow from the same causes. Ambition, avarice, self-
love, vanity, friendship, generosity, public spirit; these passions,
mixed in various degrees, and distributed through society, have
been, from the beginning of the world, and still are, the source of
all the actions and enterprises, which have ever been observed
among mankind. (8.7 / 83)

The conjunction between motives and voluntary actions is as
regular and uniform, as that between the cause and effect in
any part of nature . . . [and] this regular conjunction has been
universally acknowledged among mankind, and has never been
the subject of dispute, either in philosophy or common life. (8.16
/ 88)

If we think about our everyday life, we find that we expect our
friends and acquaintances to act in the way that they have regularly
acted in the past.

No one has ever pretended to deny, that we can draw inferences
concerning human actions, and that those inferences are founded
on the experienced union of like actions, with like motives, inclinations, and circumstances. (8.27 / 97)

Andrea will be a sore loser at badminton tonight because she always
has been before (and she always loses). Given Hume's account of
necessity, such behaviour should be seen as necessitated and causal.
Events of type *A* (Andrea losing) and events of type *B* (Andrea
sulking) have been constantly conjoined in the past, and this regularity has led me to expect that *B*'s will continue to follow *A*'s. This
is all that causality and necessity amount to, and thus, Andrea's
sulks are caused and necessitated by her losing.

Hume offers various examples of where human action is taken to
be as regular as the behaviour of the physical world. First, a prisoner
who wishes to escape from jail may decide to dig through stone
rather than try and persuade his guards to set him free. The guards
are more inflexible than the walls of his cell; their past behaviour
suggests that the prisoner is more likely to move stone with physical
force than he is to move the guards with psychological persuasion.
Second, if a prisoner is executed, his death is as much the result of

the regular and predictable action of the executioner as it is of the sharp axe (8.19 / 90). Third, people are consistently covetous of wealth, and we would expect an unattended bag of gold in a busy street to be pilfered; we expect this to happen to the bag of gold with as much confidence as we expect that it will not float away like a feather (8.20 / 91). Both expectations are the result of our experience of past regularities. And lastly:

> A manufacturer reckons upon the labour of his servants, for the execution of any work, as much as upon the tools, which he employs, and would be equally surprized, were his expectations disappointed. (8.17 / 89)

Of course we are not always sure how a certain person will act, but this is also so with respect to the behaviour of the physical world. Empirical expectations are based on probabilities, and the confidence we have in a certain event occurring is proportional to how regularly it has happened in the past. My snowdrops usually bloom in February, and Iain usually goes out on Friday nights. These events do not always occur, but I expect that they will with roughly the same confidence. The fact that such occurrences are not uniformly regular is not because the behaviour of my snowdrops and Iain are sometimes outside the influence of causality and necessity; it is, rather, because we are ignorant of the causal relations that hold in those cases that go against the norm. We make various predictions concerning the weather because we assume it is 'governed by steady principles' (8.15 / 88). Sometimes, though, we are surprised by the turn the weather takes. This, however, is because there are causal factors of which we are not aware; there is a 'secret opposition of contrary causes' (8.13 / 87). Similarly, my snowdrops may not bloom in February because weevils have eaten the bulbs. In every case it turns out that 'upon an exact scrutiny, a contrariety of effects always betrays a contrariety of causes' (8.13 / 87), and thus:

> The irregular events, which outwardly discover themselves, can be no proof, that the laws of nature are not observed with the greatest regularity . . . (8.14 / 87)

So too with people. We expect a normally obliging person to continue to be so, but there are times when he is 'peevish'. This is not because his actions are not necessitated, but because he has a toothache or he has not dined (8.15 / 88). Similarly, Iain did not go out last Friday night as he usually does because he had food poisoning. We could therefore confidently predict *all* human action if we were:

> Perfectly acquainted with every circumstance of our situation and temper, and the most secret springs of our complexion and disposition. (8.22, fn. 18 / 94, fn.)

History also reveals to us the universal occurrence of such regularities in human behaviour.

> [History's] chief use is only to discover the constant and universal principles of human nature, by showing men in all varieties of circumstances and situations, and furnishing us with materials, from which we may form our observations, and become acquainted with the regular springs of human action and behaviour. These records of wars, intrigues, factions, and revolutions, are so many collections of experiments, by which the politician or moral philosopher fixes the principles of his science; in the same manner as the physician or natural philosopher becomes acquainted with the nature of plants, minerals, and other external objects, by the experiments, which he forms concerning them. (8.7 / 83–4)

Further, the study of history would be impossible if we did not have such expectations concerning human action. There may be certain cultural differences between us and the Trojans, but we would not understand their actions at all if we did not share with them certain fundamental motives and ways of acting, ways of acting that we have discerned in the regular behaviour of our fellows. History is only credible given our expectations of regular human action. As with history, so too with politics, the penal system, and literature. Legislation and punishment only make sense if it is assumed that they will cause people to act in a law-abiding way. And an author's portrayal of his characters is measured against our experience of how people regularly act and of how their actions follow from their motives and the particular circumstances that they are in. Literature that did not respect such regularities in human behaviour would not be good literature, and it could not be seen as describing recognizable human action.

Hume has argued that all human action is causally necessitated. This is not something that we know a priori, but something that we have learnt from experience. He accepts, though, that our actions can be 'free', and in the following section we shall see how he can allow this to be so.

b. Hume's compatibilism

The causal origin of human action would seem to be at odds with the claim that our actions are free, or so many philosophers have thought. As physical, flesh and blood creatures we are governed by the laws of nature, and thus, all our actions are causally determined. I shall now type a 'T' on my keyboard. This action was caused by the movement of muscles and tendons in my fingers. These movements themselves are the result of preceding events in my body and nervous system. Given these particular events, I was caused to move my fingers in that specific way; I was therefore caused to type a 'T' and not, say, a 'Y' or an 'R'. This kind of causal determination would seem to be incompatible with freedom, and with the claim that I freely chose to type a 'T'. If causal determination is true, then I could not have done anything but type a 'T' at that particular time.

There are two kinds of incompatibilist who accept these conclusions. Libertarians claim that our actions are not necessitated, and that irregularities in our behaviour are not always explained by contrary causes. Voluntary actions are those that we *will* to occur, and our will is not constrained by the causal laws of nature; in acting freely we violate these laws. Our will may have a causal effect on our motives and desires and consequently on our actions, but the operations of the will itself are uncaused; it exerts its influence from outside the causal flow of nature (we can call this 'metaphysical free will'). Hume, however, argues that this is not coherent. If the actions of the will are uncaused, then '[such] liberty, when opposed to necessity, not to constraint, is the same thing with chance; which is universally allowed to have no existence' (8.25 / 96). 'Everybody' (that is, most eighteenth-century philosophers) accepts that all events have a cause – it is 'universally allowed' – and thus the libertarian position is untenable. The kind of liberty that is opposed to Humean necessity can only amount to arbitrariness or chaos, and Hume's arguments in Part 1 of this section should have persuaded us that our actions are not free in this sense since they are regular and predictable.

Like libertarians, 'hard determinists' also claim that causal determination is incompatible with freedom. They, however, maintain determinism at the cost of denying that our actions are free. The libertarian and hard determinist positions are responses to the 'problem of determinism': the problem being that liberty and causal determination seem to be incompatible with each other even though it is plausible that they are both features of human action. Hume, though, argues that these commitments are compatible: an action can be both free and determined, and in order to see how this can be so, we must have a proper understanding of freedom and causal necessitation. Hume claims that 'a few intelligible definitions would immediately have put an end to the whole controversy' (8.2 / 81) – that is, the problem of determinism – and that 'the whole controversy has hitherto turned merely on words' (8.3 / 81). He does not mean to imply that the problem is trivial or unimportant. Far from it: it concerns our very nature as free moral beings. The claim is that his reconciling strategy involves getting clear on the meaning of the terms 'necessity' and 'liberty'. If we have a clear understanding of these notions, and if we think carefully about what we actually take liberty and necessity to be, then we shall see that they are compatible.

We have already looked at Hume's account of causation and necessity; let us now turn to his conception of liberty. Liberty is:

A power of acting or not acting, according to the determinations of the will; that is, if we choose to remain at rest, we may; if we choose to move, we also may. Now this hypothetical liberty is universally allowed to belong to every one, who is not a prisoner and in chains. Here then is no subject of dispute. (8.23 / 95)

Liberty is contrasted with constraint rather than with necessity. I am not free if I am physically constrained: if, for example, I am tied up or locked in a room. I am free, though, if I am not restrained from doing what I choose to do. Free actions may therefore be caused by our motives and desires, and they may perhaps be totally predictable; nevertheless, they are free if they are physically unconstrained. Iain is caused to go to the pub on Friday by his desire for beer, and I predict that he is going to go there because he has regularly done so in the past. Further, Iain's motives, desires and will could all ultimately be determined by the laws of nature; nevertheless, he is still free because he does what he chooses to do (even though he may have no control over his choices; he may be caused to choose one course of action rather than another). Such compatibilism is also called 'soft determinism' since the impact of determinism is softened by the claim that causally determined action can also be seen as free.

c. Problems with Hume's compatibilism
1. I could have done something else
Some philosophers claim that part of what it means to be free is that I could have done something else in any given situation; there are alternative courses of action open to me. I have just scratched my leg because it itches; I need not, though, have done that: I could have done something else instead. This, however, is not so according to Hume. My desire to stop the itching causes me to scratch my leg. There may not be causal powers driving my behaviour, but, as argued, Humean necessity is a feature of human action.

> The conjunction between motives and voluntary actions is as regular and uniform, as that between the cause and effect in any part of nature . . . (8.16 / 88)

I do not always scratch my leg when it itches, but this is because there is sometimes a 'secret opposition of contrary causes'; perhaps I have a desire not to be seen acting in such an indelicate manner. But, given the psychological state I was just in, and the particular set of circumstances that obtained, my scratching was necessitated.

Hume acknowledges that we sometimes *feel* that there are alternative possibilities open to us.

> We feel, that our actions are subject to our will, on most occasions; and imagine we feel, that the will itself is subject to nothing, because, when by a denial of it we are provoked to try, we feel, that it moves easily every way, and produces an image of itself . . . even on that side, on which it did not settle. This image, or faint motion, we persuade ourselves, could, at that time, have been compleated into the thing itself . . . (8.22, fn. 18 / 94, fn.)

According to Hume, though, we are wrong: this is merely 'a false sensation or seeming experience which we have, or may have, of liberty or indifference, in many of our actions.' (8.22, fn. 18 / 94, fn.)

But is Hume's conception of liberty adequate? The objection here is that it does not allow for the possibility that we could – at any particular moment – do something else instead. And thus, Kant claims that Hume's strategy 'is a wretched subterfuge with which some persons allow themselves to be put off, and so think that they have solved, with a petty word jugglery, a problem at the solution of which centuries have laboured in vain' (Kant 1788: 189–90).

2. Compulsive behaviour

A key distinction for Hume is that between the internal and external causes of our behaviour. I am free if my actions are caused by my will (an internal cause). My freedom, however, can be contravened by external physical causes that constrain my actions. There is a problem here for Hume in that the internal/external distinction does not provide a correct classification of actions into those that are free and those that are not. Certain individuals do not act freely because they are constrained by internal (psychological) causes and not by ones that are external. Some kleptomaniacs want to steal, although they may wish they did not have such desires. According to Hume's account such people act freely because their will is to steal and that is what they do. But this does not seem right. These are people who are driven by their compulsive desires, desires they wish they did not have, and desires that are not under their control. If they could be 'cured' of these compulsions, then they would be able to act freely. Richard Taylor (1974: 45–6) also considers the case of the ingenious physiologist. Imagine that this scientist attaches all sorts of wires to your brain and is able to induce in you various volitions. He can make you want to lift up your arm, type a 'T', or scratch your leg. And when you have such volitions, you act on them. On Hume's account these actions are free because you act *'according to the determinations of the will'*. But surely not: you are merely the physiologist's puppet; you are not in control, just as the kleptomaniac may not be in control of his actions.

There may, however, be room for a broadly Humean account that allows for such cases. Hume claims that liberty is opposed to constraint and not necessity, and thus, Hume requires an account of the relevant constraints that limit our freedom. These must include, as Hume argues, external physical constraints such as a prisoner's chains, but also, internal psychological ones such as compulsions and addictions, and those induced by the manipulations of ingenious physiologists.

d. Morality

In Part 2 of Section 8 Hume supports his compatibilism by arguing that:

> The doctrines, both of necessity and of liberty . . . are not only consistent with morality, but are absolutely essential to its support. (8.26 / 97)

We place moral value on people's actions: we see certain of them as good, laudable or praiseworthy, and others as bad, evil or wretched. And, our actions can only be morally assessed in this way if they are performed freely. If a prisoner is forced at gunpoint to beat one of his fellows, then he is not responsible for his actions, and he should not be seen as acting poorly. Actions caused by external factors (or chance) reveal nothing about the moral standing of the agent. If I am to be responsible for a certain action – and if that action can therefore be morally assessed – then it must have been my free choice to act in that way.

Morally significant actions must therefore be caused by something in the agent herself; only then can they be seen as *her* fault or as something for which *she* deserves praise. Again, Hume does not claim that agents have intelligible causal powers, or that their actions are necessitated in the metaphysical sense; there is no justification for believing that such causation exists in the physical world or in the minds and bodies of thinkers. His claim is that there must be constant conjunctions between people's motives and their actions, and that such regularities cause others to expect them to keep on acting in the way that they have before. Hume also adds that the motives upon which we act must be the product of our character; our actions must proceed from 'some *cause* in the character and disposition of the person who performed them' (8.29 / 98). You should not be morally praised or blamed for an action if you perform it 'ignorantly and casually', or if it did not originate in a character trait 'that is durable and constant'. Actions that can be assessed as morally praiseworthy or reprehensible are those that reflect our underlying character.

Hume has argued that actions only have a moral dimension if they are performed freely and if their causal origin lies in aspects of an agent's character. He also has a naturalistic story that explains why both liberty and causal necessity are essential for morality. We do not *reason* or *conclude* that a person deserves praise because he acts out of his good character; we cannot, therefore, *justify* our moral verdicts. It is simply that:

> The mind of man is so formed by nature, that, upon the appearance of certain characters, dispositions, and actions, it immediately feels the sentiment of approbation and blame . . . (8.35 / 102)

A good action is one that causes us to feel 'approbation', and to act reprehensibly is to act in the kind of way that causes others to feel 'blame' towards you. We expect our fellows to continue to act in the way that they always have, and we infer that their regular actions are caused by their motives and desires, mental states that are a product of their character. This is the same kind of expectation and inference that occurs with respect to the physical world. I expect my snowdrops to bloom, and I infer that their doing so is caused by the germination of their bulbs. With each other, however, such inferences are accompanied by moral sentiments or feelings. When I infer that a person's behaviour is caused by his bad character, I also *feel* that he is to blame. There are therefore two ways in which Humean necessity is essential to morality. First, constant conjunctions are required between character traits, motives and actions; moral sentiments are only generated if there are such regularities. Second, these sentiments are a product of the mechanics of the mind, and, for Hume, such machinations simply consist in constant conjunctions between types of ideas, impressions and feelings.

The fact that liberty is essential to morality can also be given a naturalistic explanation. We are only caused to feel moral sentiments when the actions we observe are not physically constrained. No reasoning is involved here; it's just a fact that moral sentiments are felt only towards a person when her circumstances are conducive to free action. Hume's picture is naturalistic because his account of morality simply looks to the kind of circumstances in which the moral sentiments are generated. These circumstances are those in which actions are physically unconstrained – i.e. free – *and* those in which a person's character is the cause of her actions. Hume's compatibilism is driven by empirical facts about our cognitive mechanisms, and about what we think and feel in response to the regular behaviour of our fellows.

Morality amounts to the feeling of moral sentiments by creatures like us, and thus, if there were no humans – or no creatures that feel sentiments in the way that we do – then there would be no morality in the world. Moral subjects are distinguished from those to whom morality does not apply, not because (as the libertarian might say) we have metaphysical free will, nor because we are made in the image of God, but because it is simply a fact about us that (most of the time) we do not feel moral sentiments towards the weather, jellyfish or word-processing packages, and yet we naturally and consistently do feel moral sentiments towards human agents that are physically uncon-strained and whose actions are caused by enduring character traits.

e. Some problems with Hume's account of morality

First, it is not clear whether persisting character traits are as import-ant to morality as Hume claims. Surely you can be blamed for some-thing even if you act out of character. Hume also claims that 'repentance wipes off every crime'; repentance being a sign that your underlying character has reformed.

> Actions render a person criminal, merely as they are proofs of criminal principles in the mind; and when, by an alteration of these principles, they cease to be just proofs, they likewise cease to be criminal. (8.30 / 99)

This doesn't seem right either, and these claims are particularly prob-lematic given Hume's naturalistic approach. It's a fact about humans that we still feel moral sentiments towards others even when their actions are not caused by enduring character traits, and we may not forgive those who repent for their crimes (although repentance may allow for some mitigation). Those who repent can still be blamed because we infer that *they* acted in a certain way, even if they have now lost some of the offending character traits that they once had. Similarly, if a person acts out of character, it is still *that person* who acts, and thus, that person who can be praised or blamed, even though she acts in a way that is inconsistent with her enduring character traits.

Second, there is a more fundamental problem with Hume's account, and one that he himself acknowledges. Hume claims that we are responsible for our actions because their causal origin lies in our desires and motives; that is, there is a constant conjunc-tion between our motives and certain types of action. However, on a naturalistic account, the cause of an action ultimately lies outside of the agent. There may, for example, be constant conjunctions between particular motives and aspects of a person's genetic inheritance or environment. A person's actions may be (in part) caused by her motives and desires, but whether or not she has these particular mental states is something that is out of her control, and thus, she is not responsible for the actions that they cause her to perform. There is therefore no place for morality in the world. As said, Hume acknowledges this problem, but he does not provide an answer to it.

> I pretend not to have obviated or removed all objections to this theory . . . It may be said, for instance, that, if voluntary actions be subjected to the same laws of necessity with the operations of matter, there is a continued chain of necessary causes, pre-ordained and pre-determined, reaching from the original cause of all, to every single volition of every human creature. No contingency anywhere in the universe; no indifference; no liberty. While we act, we are, at the same time, acted upon. (8.32 / 99)

Hume has an ambitious goal: nothing short of a secular, naturalistic account of the nature of personal freedom, of our place in the causal order of nature, and of the basis of morality. We are free, not in the sense that our actions are independent of the laws of nature, but because, at times, we can act according to our will and unfettered by physical constraints. We are moral creatures because our cognitive mechanisms lead us to feel moral sentiments towards the actions of our fellows. It is crucial to note that there is no mention of God in either Hume's account of metaphysics or morality; a descriptive naturalistic psychology is all that is required. This secular theme continues in the following sections and, as has been suggested, it is the driving theme of his whole *Enquiry*.

Questions
1. 'Reflect . . . on the character of the experiences you have as you engage in normal, everyday ordinary . . . actions. You will sense the possibility of alternative courses of action built into those experiences. Raise your arm or walk across the room or take a drink of water, and you will see that at any point in the experience you have a sense of alternative courses of action open to you' (Searle 1984: 95). What would Hume say about such experience?
2. If determinism is true, then in principle it is possible for everything I do to be predicted in advance. However, if a scientist (or

God) makes any such prediction, I always have the option to go and do something else instead. Determinism is therefore false. What would Hume say about this argument?

3. How can Hume claim that our actions are necessitated (or determined) when he has argued that we have no reason to think that past regularities will continue to hold? There must be a sense in which alternative courses of action are open to us since *anything* could happen next: the sun may not rise tomorrow and I may not yawn (as I have always done at this time of night).

4. Bill is a heroin addict who hates himself for being so addicted. He constantly tries to kick the habit, yet fails. Ben is also an addict but enjoys being so; he has no intention to quit. Do Bill and Ben exercise their free will in using heroin? Can Hume's account of free will provide a plausible description of their actions?

9. OF THE REASON OF ANIMALS

This short section of the *Enquiry* is often overlooked. This, however, is a mistake: Hume's views on animals are key to understanding his overall naturalistic philosophy, and the radical nature of his claims – to his contemporaries, and still to many people today – should not be underestimated.

Traditionally humans are seen to hold a special place in the natural order of things, a place higher than that of animals. Some philosophers have claimed that this is because we have a cognitive insight into the nature of the world that animals lack. Through a priori reasoning alone we can come to know truths about the nature of the world. We can know, for example, that every event has a cause, and that God exists. Such insight is a product of our 'understanding' or 'reason'. And:

> It is the *Understanding* that sets Man above the rest of sensible Beings, and gives him all the Advantage and Dominion which he has over them. (Locke 1689: I.I.1)
>
> [Reason is] that faculty whereby Man is supposed to be distinguished from Beasts, and wherein it is evident he much surpasses them. (Locke 1689: IV.XVII.1)

These powers of reasoning place us above animals and nearer to God in the natural order, or in 'the great chain of being' (Lovejoy

1936). They can also be taken as supporting the popular Enlightenment idea that we are made in the image of God.

Hume's philosophy is completely at odds with this picture. First, we do not have rational or cognitive insight into the essential nature of the world. We have seen this with respect to causation. There is no epistemic justification for belief in causal powers; such belief is instead explained in terms of mechanistic psychological processes resulting from our regular experience. Second, we are not made in the image of God. Our powers of reasoning are not a reflection of the divine which raise us above a merely animal existence. We are just another part of the natural world – another mechanism within it – and the difference between animal and human thought is one of degree. We may be a highly developed species of animal, but we are animal nonetheless, and we can be studied as other animals can using the scientific experimental method. God-like rational insight is replaced by cognitive processes under the control of a mechanistically conceived imagination, the kind of processes that also govern animal thinking. Further, in Sections 10 and 11, Hume claims that there is no justification for belief in the Christian God. We do not have God-like reasoning – whatever that might consist of – and there is no reason to think that God exists.

Hume argues by analogy. Animal behaviour is similar to our own in various ways, and such similarities suggest that animals have certain experiences and ways of thinking in common with man.

> Animals undoubtedly feel, think, love, hate, will, and even reason. (Hume 1996: 325)
>
> No truth appears to me more evident, than that the beasts are endow'd with thought and reason as well as men. The arguments are in this case so obvious, that they never escape the most stupid and ignorant. (Hume 1739–40: 176)

The key claim here is that animals 'reason'. This is 'obvious' because they clearly learn from experience and their expectations are conditioned by past constant conjunctions.

> Animals, as well as men, learn many things from experience, and infer, that the same events will always follow from the same causes. (9.2 / 105)

> The animal infers some fact beyond what immediately strikes his senses; and this inference is altogether founded on past experience . . . (9.4 / 106)

This kind of cognition is based on what Hume calls causal reasoning, and, since animals are merely part of the natural world, there is a naturalistic explanation for it. Such thinking does not depend on chains of reasoning or argument, or on a semi-divine spark of understanding or reason; it is more primitive: it is instinctive or habitual. This does not mean that animals have some kind of sub-human intelligence; quite the contrary since Hume has argued that *our* empirical reasoning is also habitual in this way. Animals therefore think in broadly the same way as we do. Given similarities in our behaviour – those that allow us to attribute experiences and thoughts to animals – the same naturalistic explanation should be given of both animal and human thought, that is, an explanation involving Hume's mechanistic account of the mind.

> The experimental reasoning itself, which we possess in common with beasts, and on which the whole conduct of life depends, is nothing but a species of instinct, or mechanical power . . . Though the instinct be different, yet still it is an instinct, which teaches a man to avoid the fire; as much as that, which teaches a bird, with such exactness, the art of incubation, and the whole oeconomy and order of its nursery. (9.6 / 108)
>
> Animals, therefore, are not guided in these inferences by reasoning: Neither are children: Neither are the generality of mankind, in their ordinary actions and conclusions: Neither are philosophers themselves . . . Nature must have provided some other principle . . . It is custom alone, which engages animals, from every object, that strikes their senses, to infer its usual attendant, and carries their imagination, from the appearance of the one, to conceive the other, in that particular manner, which we denominate *belief*. No other explication can be given of this operation, in all the higher, as well as lower classes of sensitive beings . . . (9.5 / 106–7)

Hume would have embraced the findings of contemporary behavioural biology. In experiments rhesus monkeys learn to pull the levers that cause their fellows to express food responses rather than shock

(Miller 1971); they therefore engage in causal reasoning, inferring that a certain lever will bring them food rather than pain. Similarly, vervet monkeys learn to react to the causal connection between cattle mooing and danger (Cheney and Seyfarth 1985). And certain baboons fool aggressors by feigning that they see a large predator in the distance; their attacker often reacts by turning to see what it is that is apparently scaring the devious baboon, thus giving him time to escape (Byrne and Whiten 1988: 132–3). Baboons have therefore learnt that their aggressive fellows have picked up on the causal connection between danger and a certain kind of behavioural response. These are not cases in which animals are merely 'programmed' to offer a simple response to a simple stimulus; these are cases in which animals have learnt a complex form of behaviour in response to environmental problems, and they have learnt to do this using Humean causal reasoning. A wasp may sting anything in its path; a stag, however, seems to decide whether to fight by weighing up his chance of success based on past encounters (Clutton-Brock and Albon 1979: 145–70). Such behaviour is very Humean: a dominant aggressive stag may not have proof that he will win, but he can infer that there is a good probability that he will (with 'proof', 'infer' and 'probability' taken in Hume's sense).

Hume does acknowledge that there are certain differences between human and animal thought (see 9.5, fn. 20 / 107, fn.). Human thought is unique in that it turns to questions of morality, law and religion. Later philosophers have come to focus on man's linguistic abilities and it is these that enable us to have such sophisticated thoughts. Hume does not consider this route, although he does note that testimony from books and conversation enlarges our experience and thus enables us to have thoughts that would be beyond an isolated individual (or a non-linguistic animal). He also suggests other naturalistic explanations for differences between animal and human thinking. First, cognitive abilities vary between people – and between people and animals – because there are differences in powers of attention and memory, and these differences in turn lead to differences in reasoning capacity. Second, 'larger' minds can more easily think about complex systems of objects and pursue longer chains of causal reasoning. For Hume, similar quantitative differences between the cognitive powers of men and animals explain why our thinking is capable of more complex operations. Third, we saw in Section 8 that thoughts concerning morality are the product of the imagination; creatures, therefore, that are not capable of thinking in moral terms are those whose minds do not mechanistically produce the requisite sentiments of 'blame and approbation'.

We have now become used to the view that we are animals and, more specifically, a close relative of the apes. It is interesting to note, though, that this modern outlook owes much to Charles Darwin and his theory of evolution by natural selection, a theory that is independent of Hume's claims concerning animal cognition. *The Origin of the Species* was published in 1859, and the fact that Darwin's theory was initially vilified and ridiculed highlights the radical nature of Hume's view given that Darwin wrote a century after the *Enquiry* was published. In the eighteenth century, even the title of Hume's discussion – 'Of the Reason of Animals' – would have goaded many readers. Of course animals cannot *reason*. Man is special because, even if he is an animal, he is the only rational animal. Hume was not averse to subtly winding up his opponents:

> The rotting of a turnip, the generation of an animal, and the structure of human thought . . . are energies that probably bear some remote analogy to each other. (Hume 1779: 218)

We are not made in the image of God, and the workings of our minds are more akin to the kind of natural biological processes involved in the rotting of a vegetable! To many eighteenth-century thinkers Hume's claims concerning animals are extremely shocking. Thinkers of the Enlightenment embraced the new sciences and great strides were being made in the study of the physiology and anatomy of our bodies. However, the Cartesian view was that our mind is not open to scientific investigation. The behaviour of animals may be given a wholly mechanistic explanation, but our behaviour is driven by a non-mechanistic mind – one that possesses metaphysical free will – and it is such a mind that is the seat of our understanding and reason. Hume rejects this picture and in many ways Section 9 of Hume's *Enquiry* encapsulates his whole world view. Neither humans nor animals have rational a priori insight into the nature of reality, and neither are fashioned in the image of God. We are both mechanistic creatures and consequently the fit subject for scientific investigation; this is so for our bodies and for our minds.

Questions

1. What would Hume say about the following claims?

It is in this same respect that man's knowledge differs from that of beasts: beasts are sheer empirics and are guided entirely by instances. While men are capable of demonstrative knowledge, beasts, so far as one can judge, never manage to form necessary propositions, since the faculty by which they make thought sequences is somewhat lower than the reason that occurs in men. Beasts' thought sequences are just like those of simple empirics who maintain that what has happened once will happen again in a case which is similar in the respects that they are impressed by, although that does not enable them to judge whether the same reasons are at work. (Leibniz 1705: 50)

2. According to Hume, what kinds of thought do my cat and I have in common, and in what ways does our thinking differ?

10. OF MIRACLES

a. Hume turns to religion

Hume now moves on to a key theme of the book, that of religion, and Sections 10 and 11 comprise a powerful attack on religious belief. 'Natural Religion' or 'Natural Theology' involves assessing whether there are compelling arguments in favour of the existence of God; Section 11 considers this approach. Section 10 focuses on 'Revealed Religion' or 'Revelation'; religious texts such as the Bible and the Qur'an describe how God reveals himself to mankind. One way of doing this is through miracles, and many people believe in God because miraculous happenings can only have a divine explanation. Hume argues that we should not believe that miracles have occurred and that they do not therefore provide us with any reason to think that God exists.

For Hume, laws of nature describe regularities in our experience; they are generalizations to which we have no counterexamples. It is a law of nature that:

All men must die; that lead cannot, of itself, remain suspended in the air; that fire consumes wood, and is extinguished by water . . . (10.12 / 114)

'A miracle is a violation of the laws of nature' (10.12 / 114). Miracles are therefore at odds with our usual run of experience and this is something which believers and doubters agree upon.

> There must . . . be a uniform experience against every miraculous event, otherwise the event would not merit that appellation. (10.12 / 115)

It is because such events are so unusual and not explainable in terms of the laws of nature that they point towards the intervention of a deity.

Miracles are distinguished from occurrences that are merely 'marvellous' or 'incredible'. It would be incredibly lucky to be dealt a royal flush at poker. This would not, however, be counter to a law of nature; it is just an event that is highly unlikely. We sometimes speak loosely and say that such unlikely events are 'miraculous', but they are not miraculous in Hume's sense. Hume is also careful to claim that miracles are not merely events that are outside a particular person's experience. An Indian prince may not believe that water freezes because that is not 'conformable with his experience' – it is novel *to him* – but it is not 'contrary' to his experience in the sense of being contrary to an established law of nature. The prince has no experience of what happens at such low temperatures and so there is nothing in his experience with which to compare such an occurrence.

b. Part 1: testimonial evidence

Hume focuses on testimony, that is, on written and spoken reports of miracles. He claims that miraculous phenomena are so unlikely that any reports concerning them should always be explained away rather than accepted. We should not believe that Jesus rose from the dead or that he turned water into wine (without using yeast). Hume claims to have:

> Discovered an argument . . . which, if just, will, with the wise and learned, be an everlasting check to all kinds of superstitious delusion, and consequently, will be useful as long as the world endures. (10.2 / 110)

Hume's argument is in two parts. In Part 1 he establishes the appropriate standards for assessing testimony in general, and then in Part 2 these are applied to the special case of miracles.

First, Hume accepts that we should sometimes believe testimonial reports because they have experiential support. If Terry has always been right about whether a particular fungus is edible, then I will expect him to be right in the future. I expect him to continue to be reliable just as I expect the sun to rise tomorrow. Of course, Hume has argued in Section 4 that there is no *justification* for thinking in this way; there are no arguments to show that such trust is warranted. Nevertheless – via instinct, custom or habit – his past record leads me to believe that he can be trusted.

> The reason, why we place any credit in witnesses and historians, is not derived from any *connexion*, which we perceive *a priori*, between testimony and reality, but because we are accustomed to find a conformity between them. (10.8 / 113)

Such reasoning from experience may not be justified but it does amount to good cognitive practice since 'experience [is] our only guide in reasoning concerning matters of fact' (10.3 / 110). From the perspective of everyday life: '[a] wise man proportions his belief to the evidence' (10.4 / 110) – and philosophical argument cannot undermine the grounds of such wisdom.

With respect to testimony there are two sources of experiential evidence that must be weighed against each other, one concerning the intrinsic likelihood of the reported event, and the other the chance that the speaker is either lying or mistaken in some way. Is this fungus likely to be edible? There are only a few poisonous species and so there is a good chance that it is not one of these. Is Terry likely to be telling the truth? Well, he has collected fungi for many years, he has nothing to gain by lying to me, and a lot to lose if he is mistaken since he always eats the fungi he collects. There is therefore only a slim chance that he is mistaken and thus I should believe what he says. There are other times, however, when it is not wise to accept someone's testimony.

> We entertain a suspicion concerning any matter of fact, when the witnesses contradict each other; when they are but few, or of a doubtful character; when they have an interest in what they affirm; when they deliver their testimony with hesitation, or on the contrary, with too violent asseverations. (10.7 / 112–13)

This way of assessing evidence is also applicable to testimony concerning miracles. We should weigh the evidence in favour of a certain law of nature continuing to hold against the testimonial evidence that a miracle has occurred. Since laws of nature describe universal regularities in our experience, there is a 'uniform experience against every miraculous event' (10.12 / 115). We therefore have a 'proof' that a miracle will not occur.

> A firm and unalterable experience has established these laws, the proof against a miracle, from the very nature of the fact, is as entire as any argument from experience can possibly be imagined. (10.12 / 114)

To counteract such evidence very persuasive testimony is required.

> No testimony is sufficient to establish a miracle, unless the testimony be of such a kind, that its falsehood would be more miraculous, than the fact, which it endeavours to establish . . . When anyone tells me, that he saw a dead man restored to life, I immediately consider with myself, whether it be more probable, that this person should either deceive or be deceived, or that the fact, which he relates, should really have happened. I weigh the one miracle against the other; and according to the superiority, which I discover, I pronounce my decision, and always reject the greater miracle. If the falsehood of his testimony would be more miraculous, than the event which he relates; then, and not till then, can he pretend to command my belief or opinion. (10.13 / 115–16)

If Karen has always identified water and wine correctly in the past, and has always been scrupulously honest, then I have a proof that she will continue to be reliable. I also have a proof that water does not transmute into wine either spontaneously or by supernatural means since this has never happened in my experience. If Karen, therefore, was to report such a transmutation, I would have to weigh 'proof against proof' (10.11 / 114). This can be done since one proof may involve more 'experiments' than another. I may have observed more stable glasses of water – those that do not transmute into wine – than I have heard relevant reports by Karen. In this case, then, the proof against a miraculous happening is stronger than that in favour. This would not have to be so if I were to believe that a miracle had occurred. The scales would have to tip the other way with a stronger proof in favour of a miracle. It is important to note that this possibility remains open; at this stage Hume has merely described the high standards that testimony concerning miracles has to meet.

c. Part 2: the empirical evidence against miracle reports
In Part 2, however, Hume presents empirical evidence to show that there has never been a report of a religious miracle that has lived up to the standards required of it, and there is never likely to be one.

> We have supposed, that the testimony, upon which a miracle is founded, may possibly amount to an entire proof, and that the falsehood of that testimony would be a real prodigy: But it is easy to show, that we have been a great deal too liberal in our concession, and that there never was a miraculous event established on so full an evidence. (10.14 / 116)

He picks out the testimony given in the first five books of the Old Testament (the Pentateuch) for particular criticism.

> I desire any one to lay his hand upon his heart, and after serious consideration declare, whether he thinks that the falsehood of such a book [the Pentateuch], supported by such a testimony, would be more extraordinary and miraculous than all the miracles it relates . . . (10.40 / 130)

He presents four arguments for the claim that a miracle report has never satisfied the requisite epistemic standard. First, historical records reveal that there has never been a sufficient number of reliable witnesses to a miracle.

> There is not to be found, in all history, any miracle attested by a sufficient number of men, of such unquestioned good sense, education, and learning, as to secure us against all delusion in themselves; of such undoubted integrity, as to place them beyond all suspicion of any design to deceive others; of such credit and reputation in the eyes of mankind, as to have a great deal to lose in case of their being detected in any falsehood; and at the same time, attesting facts, performed in such a public manner, and in so celebrated a part of the world, as to render the detection unavoidable. (10.15 / 116–17)

History reveals a catalogue of forged miracles and fabricated holy relics. The long history of religious corruption gives us reason to think that in any particular case we may be being conned. Hume's first claim, then, rests on whether his assessment of the historical evidence is correct. Was there, for example, a 'sufficient number' of witnesses to the resurrection? And did they have the required impartiality and integrity?

Second, there are various psychological factors that suggest we are gullible when it comes to miracles. Many people have an intense desire that religious teachings are true and, particularly, that there is the possibility of life after death. Such desires can lead to self-deception, and our usual ways of thinking can be subverted by 'enthusiasm'. In a mobile-phone shop we may be alert to the trickery of the salesmen, but when it comes to religion we may lose our usual good sense and critical faculties. Hume claims that:

> If the spirit of religion join itself to the love of wonder, then there is an end of common sense; and human testimony, in these circumstances, loses all pretensions to authority. (10.17 / 117)
>
> But when anything is affirmed utterly absurd and miraculous . . . [t]he passion of *surprize* and *wonder*, arising from miracles, being an agreeable emotion, gives a sensible tendency towards the belief of those events, from which it is derived. And this goes so far, that even those who cannot enjoy the pleasure immediately, nor can believe those miraculous events, of which they are informed, yet love to partake of the satisfaction at second-hand or by rebound, and place a pride and delight in exciting the admiration of others. (10.16 / 117)

It is pleasing to us to find that the world is not a totally regular and mechanical place, and our vanity is massaged if we can report miraculous happenings to our fellows: 'But what greater temptation than to appear a missionary, a prophet, an ambassador from heaven?' (10.29 / 125) And, 'with what greediness are the miraculous accounts of travellers received' (10.17 / 117).

> The smallest spark may here kindle into the greatest flame; because the materials are always prepared for it . . . the gazing populace, receive greedily, without examination, whatever sooths superstition, and promotes wonder. (10.30 / 126)

Hume's claim is that there is empirical evidence that when it comes to miracles people are gullible and vain. This reduces the probability that their testimony is correct and should therefore lead us to doubt that miracles have occurred (given that we have an entire proof that the laws of nature will continue to hold).

To Hume this is common sense. Even if your best friend claims to see an angel you should not believe her. She may have seen something that looked like an angel, but she did not see a real angel, a creature that in various ways contravenes the laws of nature. There is always more chance that she was mistaken in some way or perhaps seduced by vanity into fabricating such a story. Even though the Stoic Cato was famed for his honesty, Hume claims that '*I should not believe such a* [miracle] *story were it told me by* CATO' (10.9 / 113). (I once found myself in an argument over this very point. I took the Humean line and claimed not to believe that a close friend had seen, in this case, a ghost. 'That's outrageous, she's your friend – how can you not believe her?' Citing Hume's argument did not get me out of trouble!)

Hume's third argument is that miracles are usually:

> Observed chiefly to abound among ignorant and barbarous nations; or if a civilized people has ever given admission to any of them, that people will be found to have received them from ignorant and barbarous ancestors . . . (10.20 / 119)

They should therefore not be looked on favourably. Again, the Pentateuch is picked out for particular criticism.

> [It is] a book, presented to us by a barbarous and ignorant people, written in an age when they were still more barbarous, and in all probability long after the facts which it relates, corroborated by no concurring testimony . . . (10.40 / 130)

And, reports of miracles:

> Grow thinner every page, in proportion as we advance nearer the enlightened ages, we soon learn, that there is nothing mysterious or supernatural in the case . . . (10.20 / 119)

There is a prejudiced air about Hume's claims here; but is there any truth in them? What does Hume mean by 'barbarous'? And how does this claim sit with the fact that miracles are regularly reported by healers in the Bible Belt of America and at Lourdes in France?

Fourth, different religions aim to justify their own teachings with miraculous happenings, but one cannot believe in the occurrence of all such miracles because various religions make contradictory claims about the world and the nature of God. 'In matters of religion, whatever is different is contrary' (10.24 / 121). Christians take miracles to indicate the existence of the Christian God: the one true God, the Holy Trinity, ruler of Heaven and Earth. The gods of other religions do not have this nature and Christians claim that they do not exist – they are 'false idols'. However, adherents of non-Christian religions also have their own favoured miracles, those they see as supporting their own particular teachings, and the testimonial evidence for these miracles is just as strong as that for the Christian God (although, according to Hume, neither have particularly strong evidence to support their views). We cannot believe all such testimony because this would lead to us holding contradictory claims about God and the world, and since Christian testimony is no more persuasive than the testimony in support of Hindu or Islamic miracles, then we have no reason to favour a particular religion's viewpoint. Thus, testimony concerning miracles can never tip the scales in favour of religious belief, because the miraculous evidence in favour of the claims of a particular religion is always outweighed by the testimony supporting the miracles of other religions.

Some religions, however, do not claim that theirs is the only true God, or that miraculous happenings must indicate the intervention of their particular deity. Early Christians thought that pagan miracles pointed to the work of devils and not God, and some polytheists are happy with there being various Gods each supported by their own tradition of miracles. Further, evidence for a miraculous happening at Lourdes need not have any bearing on the evidence for such a happening at Mecca, that is, if such happenings are simply considered as transgressions of the laws of nature. Miracles, in themselves, do not have to be seen as specific to a particular religion; they can nevertheless provide us with reason to think that there is occasional supernatural intervention in the day to day course of events (with the nature of that intervention left open). However, even if this is so, Hume can still argue that miraculous happenings cannot be taken as *Christian* miracles or as *Muslim* miracles, not, that is, unless one has other reasons to think that a particular religion is correct.

Hume claims, first, that the historical evidence for miracles is poor. Second, even if the evidence were better, people are just too gullible when it comes to wondrous happenings for their testimony to be taken seriously. Third, what evidence there is has its roots in cultures without the requisite enlightened view of the world. And fourth, miracles cannot be taken as supporting a particular religion because of the anthropological fact that there are various religions in the world that hold contradictory views. Hume's conclusion is that:

> We may establish it as a maxim, that no human testimony can have such force as to prove a miracle, and make it a just foundation for any such system of religion. (10.35 / 127)

d. Miracles are not impossible

Hume does not claim that miracles are impossible, and he is explicit about this:

> There may possibly be miracles, or violations of the usual course of nature, of such a kind as to admit of proof from human testimony . . . (10.36 / 127)

His claim is only that we have not found any good testimonial evidence for them, and that the standards any future testimony must meet are very high.

First, miracles are not conceptually impossible, that is, they are not ruled out by definition. Some philosophers have interpreted Hume as making such an a priori claim. A miracle is defined as a violation of the laws of nature, yet Hume takes the laws of nature to be exceptionless regularities supported by our 'uniform experience'. Since a law of nature is exceptionless – by definition – there cannot be miraculous occurrences that provide exceptions to such laws. This is an odd interpretation of Hume given his naturalistic approach and his claim that matters of fact cannot be established a priori. And, any such interpretation can be seen as ungrounded if we note that the laws of nature are not defined as generalizations that will never be contravened, but rather, as those which have invariably held in our experience.

Second, Hume accepts that miracles are not only logically possible, but they are also empirically possible, and he goes on to describe the kind of evidence that would rightly lead us to believe in the occurrence of one.

Suppose, all authors, in all languages, agree, that, from the first of JANUARY 1600, there was a total darkness over the whole earth for eight days: Suppose that the tradition of this extraordinary event is still strong and lively among the people: That all travellers, who return from foreign countries, bring us accounts of the same tradition, without the least variation or contradiction . . . (10.36 / 127–8)

This would appear to be a miracle since a law of nature is contravened, the law of nature that the sun always rises. It is suggested that there could be widespread, consistent and ostensibly reliable reports concerning the occurrence of such a phenomenon over the whole Earth. The witnesses to such an event may be competent, honest, reliable and have no motivation to lie. If this were so, 'it is evident, that our present philosophers, instead of doubting the fact, ought to receive it as certain' (10.36 / 128). This does not, however, open the door to biblical miracles since the quality of evidence for them is not as good.

Hume goes on to distinguish the eight days of darkness case from that of a secular miracle involving the resurrection of Queen Elizabeth I. In the former case Hume introduces another factor into our probabilistic assessment of testimonial evidence.

The decay, corruption, and dissolution of nature, is an event rendered probable by so many analogies, that any phaenomenon, which seems to have a tendency towards that catastrophe, comes within the reach of human testimony, if that testimony be very extensive and uniform. (10.36 / 128)

There are other analogous examples of decay and corruption in nature that add to the probability that the usual cycle of night and day could break down; Hume may have unusual tide patterns in mind, those out of line with the normal cycle, or cases where there are freak weather conditions for a certain time of the year. There are, however, no such analogies in support of resurrection, and the mortality of man and every living creature has been found to be universal. (This example is daring since it concerns resurrection, the resurrection of Christ being a cornerstone of Christianity. Hume is subtly suggesting that we should not believe that Christ rose from the dead; the biblical reports of the resurrection do not therefore provide us with good reason to accept Christianity.)

There may appear to be some tension between Hume's attitude

to miracles and his scepticism concerning empirical reasoning. He argues that we should weigh the likelihood of a law of nature continuing to hold against the likelihood that a certain miracle report is correct. According to Hume, though, we are not justified in believing either that the world will continue to behave in the same way or that a reporter will continue to be reliable. We have no reason to think that the sun will rise tomorrow or that Cato will continue to tell the truth. And, believing that the world will continue to be a regular place has no more rational support than believing that the laws of nature will be contravened. For Hume, one course of events cannot be seen as any more likely than another and so it is not open to him to use probabilities in his argument against miracles.

Hume's position, however, is coherent and we can see how by reminding ourselves of his naturalistic approach. He has claimed that our belief in a regular world cannot be supported by argument; nevertheless, we do expect the world to go on in the same way and this is because certain habits have been inculcated in us by our regular experience. Hume's conclusions are sceptical, but he also provides a naturalistic explanation of our inductive beliefs. His account of miracles and testimony is part of this picture. Believing the testimony of a usually reliable reporter is not rationally justified; it is just something that creatures like us habitually do. Our imagination – the faculty involved in belief acquisition – is sensitive to the relative frequencies of aspects of our experience, and this is how our minds should work when viewed from the everyday perspective. In everyday situations people do weigh up the chances of testimony being correct in the way that Hume describes. However, when miracles are involved our usual instinctive mechanisms can go wrong. Our imagination is led astray by feelings of surprise, wonder and vanity.

e. The miracle of faith

Some philosophers argue that Hume is merely concerned with attacking Catholic 'superstitions' and that he does not object to Protestantism or to Christianity in general. Various reasons are offered for this claim including Hume's remark at the beginning of Section 10 that he has 'discovered an argument of a like nature' to that provided by Dr Tillotson (the Protestant Archbishop of Canterbury). The closing paragraph of this section also suggests to some that Hume accepts that there may after all be miracles, and that the miracle of religious faith can justify religious belief (faith rather than argument or revelation is an important aspect of the Protestant approach to religion).

> Mere reason is insufficient to convince us of its veracity [that of Christianity]: And whoever is moved by *Faith* to assent to it, is conscious of a continued miracle in his own person, which subverts all the principles of his understanding, and gives him a determination to believe what is most contrary to custom and experience. (10.41 / 131)

However, this passage is clearly humorous and rather barbed: it is a 'miracle' that people still follow Christianity given the paucity of the evidence for its teachings. Anthony Flew describes the end of this section as containing 'three of the most mordantly derisive sentences Hume ever wrote' (Flew 1961: 216). Throughout this section there are various digs at religion, sometimes only thinly disguised, and the tone is rather mocking: for example, I find it hard not to read the 'etc.' in the following footnote as sarcastic.

> For that miracle was really performed by the touch of an authentic holy prickle of the holy thorn, which composed the holy crown, which, etc. (10.27, fn. 25 / 346)

Hume's attitude to religious miracles is unequivocal:

> All the testimony which ever was really given for any miracle, or ever will be given, is a subject of derision. (Hume 1932: 349)

His argument is not just aimed at Catholicism and it does not just concern the miracles in the Bible. In Protestant churches today there are regular reports of miraculous healings and only last year a worldwide call was put out to Catholics to look for evidence of a miracle performed by Pope John Paul II (this is required in order that he can be classed as a saint). Hume would not spend too much time looking for such evidence since:

> Every relation must be considered as suspicious, which depends in any degree upon religion . . . And no less so, every thing that is to be found in the writers of natural magic or alchimy, or such

authors, who seem, all of them, to have an unconquerable appetite for falsehood and fable. (10.39 / 129)

In the following section we shall look further at the scope and strength of Hume's case against religious belief.

Questions

1. How do you square the following quotation with the claim that Hume does not take miracles to be *impossible*?

There surely never was a greater number of miracles ascribed to one person, than those, which were lately said to have been wrought in FRANCE upon the tomb of Abbé PARIS . . . [M]any of the miracles were immediately proved upon the spot, before judges of unquestioned integrity, attested by witnesses of credit and distinction, in a learned age, and on the most eminent theatre that is now in the world . . . And what have we to oppose to such a cloud of witnesses, but the *absolute impossibility* or miraculous nature of events, which they relate? And this surely, in the eyes of all reasonable people, will alone be regarded as a sufficient refutation. (10.27 / 124–5; our emphasis)

2. Is it contradictory to claim, as Hume does, both that miracles are possible, and that no one has ever had a justified belief that one has occurred?

3. How do the following claims affect Hume's argument concerning miracles?

(i)   There is not 'a *uniform* experience against every miraculous event' because some kinds of miracle are repeated. There have, for example, been numerous reports of resurrections in various traditions.

(ii)   People take particular care when reporting unusual and unexpected occurrences; reports of miracles are therefore likely to be more reliable than those concerning mundane everyday events.

(iii) Some of the witnesses to biblical miracles had a lot to lose – i.e. their lives – in claiming that they had seen Christ performing miracles.

4. A scientist publishes the results of a certain experiment in a scientific journal. She argues that her experimental data entails that

a presumed law of nature does not actually hold. According to Hume, should we accept this scientist's testimony? (Note that her data is at odds with our 'uniform experience' up until now.)

5. Is the following a good objection to Hume's argument concerning miracles?

> I cannot see how Hume can distinguish between our variously caused beliefs about matters of fact, and call some of them justifiable and others unjustifiable . . . The [religious] enthusiast's belief in miracles and Hume's belief in natural laws (and consequent disbelief in miracles) stand on precisely the same logical footing. In both cases we can see the psychological cause of the belief, but in neither can Hume give us any logical ground for it. We see, then, that Hume is really inconsistent in preferring a belief in the laws of nature based on constant experience to a belief in miracles based on a love of the wonderful . . . On his own theories he has no right to talk about what we ought to believe as to matters of fact. For what we ought to believe means what we are logically justified in believing, and Hume has said that he can find no logical justification for belief about matters of fact. (Broad 1916–17: 91–2)

11. OF A PARTICULAR PROVIDENCE AND OF A FUTURE STATE

In Section 10 Hume is concerned with revealed religion, and he argues that alleged miracles should not be seen as providing evidence for the existence of God. In Section 11 he turns his attention to natural religion and to those who present a particular kind of argument in support of their religious beliefs. This section is a critique of the argument from design.

a. The concealment of Hume's anti-Christian views

The content of Hume's arguments concerning religion are not immediately transparent, and his own views are somewhat masked. Hume is anti-Christian but, at the time, it would not have been wise to advertise this fact. In 1733 Thomas Woolston was tried, convicted for blasphemy, and imprisoned for four years because in his *Discourses on the Miracles of Our Saviour* he had claimed that the biblical evidence for Christ's resurrection was unreliable. Diderot was put in prison in 1746 for publishing various controversial works including *Pensées Philosophiques*; he was only released when he promised 'to do nothing in future which is any way contrary to religion or morality' (Diderot 1955: 96). And, in 1753, Peter Annet was similarly imprisoned for blasphemous libel. Sensibly, then, Hume mostly omitted religion from his *Treatise*. In the *Enquiry*, though, he is bolder. The message of Section 10 is clear enough if we are able to see through a little irony and sarcasm. In Section 11 his views are also clearly opposed to traditional Christian belief, although, again, somewhat masked.

This section is written as a dialogue between the author and a friend. They are discussing Epicurus, an ancient philosopher who denied the existence of the Roman Gods and the possibility of life after death; their debate concerns whether his views are a threat to political authority, morality and religion. The author's friend speaks on behalf of Epicurus, defends his position on moral grounds, and argues against the 'religious philosophers'. Hume's own views are disguised by the dialogue form (whose side is he on?), and by the fact that the discussion ostensibly concerns the supreme Roman God Jupiter and not Christianity. However, a natural interpretation takes the author's friend as speaking for Hume as well as for Epicurus, and the discussion as alluding to the God of Christianity.

The title of this section could also be a little obscure to the modern reader. 'Providence' refers to God's control over the universe; his general providence is over the physical laws – he sustains them – and his 'particular providence' concerns individuals: God watches over and cares for the human race. A 'future state' refers to heaven. This title could suggest that Hume is merely concerned with the evidence for such providence and for there being 'future' rewards for those who deserve them. This is somewhat misleading. The concerns of this section are wider: Hume's intention is to question whether there is any reason to believe in the Christian God at all.

God's existence is discussed in the context of certain political and social questions. Epicurus' views are condemned for:

Loosen[ing], in a great measure, the ties of morality, and may be supposed, for that reason, pernicious to the peace of civil society. (11.4 / 133–4)

Epicurus – and Hume – argue that this is not so. A godless society or a godless individual can nevertheless be good. As we saw in Section 8, morality does not depend on God or religion. Hume provides a naturalistic account of the genesis of our moral beliefs. This section does concern these moral and political issues, but, as said, it is also a direct attack on religious belief in general. Hume's intentions are clear but, for prudential reasons, they are somewhat obscured. In Hume's time it was dangerous explicitly to deny the resurrection (one of the miracles referred to in Section 10) and the existence of God, and it would be an extremely rash thing for a man of affairs like Hume to do. (Such claims are still considered by many to be highly controversial and imprudent. How many politicians, teachers, and community leaders have you heard publicly claiming that the resurrection of Jesus is fiction, or that there is no good reason to believe in the Christian God?)

b. The argument from design

Hume focuses on the argument from design because for his contemporaries this was the 'chief or sole argument for a divine existence' (11.11 / 135). In refuting this argument he therefore aims to defeat the most defensible form of natural religion. Some philosophers attempt to prove that God exists using a priori arguments. Hume has no truck with such philosophy. The argument from design, however, is an empirical argument and would therefore seem to involve the kind of reasoning of which Hume approves. The argument is as follows.

> The religious philosophers . . . paint, in the most magnificent colours, the order, beauty, and wise arrangement of the universe; and then ask, if such a glorious display of intelligence could proceed from the fortuitous concourse of atoms, or if chance could produce what the greatest genius can never sufficiently admire. (11.10 / 135)
>
> [The argument] . . . is derived from the order of nature; where there appear such marks of intelligence and design, that you think it extravagant to assign for its cause, either chance, or the blind and unguided force of matter. You allow that this is an argument drawn from effects to causes. From the order of the work, you infer, that there must have been project and forethought in the workman. (11.11 / 135–6)

Plants and animals have intricately constructed bodies that perform specific functions essential for their continuing survival, and the heavenly bodies move in concert with each other in a way that enables such motion to be perpetuated and allows life on Earth to flourish. Such order in the universe could not have come about by chance and it must therefore have been put there by God who designed the universe to be this way. The regular movement of stars in the solar system is akin to the mechanical movements of a clock, and it is easy to see the various parts of the human body as finely tuned mechanisms or instruments. This structural and functional similarity to man-made objects suggests that natural objects must also be the product of deliberate and intelligent design. It is this argument that Epicurus and Hume attack.

Hume argues that the traditional God of Christianity cannot be inferred from the order we find in nature.

> When we infer any particular cause from an effect, we must proportion the one to the other, and can never be allowed to ascribe to the cause any qualities, but what are exactly sufficient to produce the effect . . . But if we ascribe to it farther qualities, or affirm it capable of producing other effects, we can only indulge the licence of conjecture, and arbitrarily suppose the existence of qualities and energies, without reason or authority. (11.12 / 136)
>
> If the cause be known only by the effect, we never ought to ascribe to it any qualities, beyond what are precisely requisite to produce the effect . . . Allowing, therefore, the gods to be the authors of the existence or order of the universe, it follows that they possess that precise degree of power, intelligence, and benevolence, which appears in their workmanship; but nothing farther can ever be proved . . . The supposition of farther attributes is mere hypothesis . . . (11.13–14 / 136–7)

The question, then, is does the order we find in nature entail the existence of an omniscient (all-knowing), omnipotent (all-powerful), and benevolent God? The answer is 'No'. First, even if it is accepted that the creation of the universe requires a designer with knowledge and power, we are only entitled to ascribe to that creator (God) the level of these attributes that can be read off from the kind of order we find in nature. And the empirical evidence only entitles us to say something rather vague about these attributes: perhaps all we can say is that such a creator must have sufficient intellect and power to create solar systems and mechanical creatures, whatever intellect and power that might require.

> [There is] no reason to ascribe to these celestial beings any perfection or any attribute, but what can be found in the present world. (11.16 / 138)

Second, there is strong empirical evidence that the universe cannot have been created by a morally good God. This objection shall be discussed in the next section.

c. The problem of evil

If the world was designed by God, then he did not do a very good job since 'we must acknowledge the reality of that evil and disorder, with which the world so much abounds' (11.17 / 138). There are moral evils such as acts perpetrated by murderers and tyrants throughout history, and there are natural evils: disease, famine, and disasters such as the Asian tsunami and Hurricane Katrina. Millions therefore have a life that is 'poor, nasty, brutish and short'. As Hume puts it in a later work:

> The whole [creation] presents nothing but the idea of a blind nature, impregnated by a great vivifying principle, and pouring forth from her lap, without discernment or parental care, her maimed and abortive children. (1779: 211–12)

The existence of such evil would appear to be incompatible with the design plan of a benevolent creator. The Christian God is omniscient, omnipotent and good, yet an omniscient God could foresee the evils that will be caused by nature and man, and an omnipotent God should, if he is good, eliminate them from the world.

Some, however, argue that the state of the world is compatible with divine creation. A 'theodicy' is an explanation of why God allows the world to contain such evil. Hume discusses four theodicies. First, 'the obstinate and intractable qualities of matter . . . or the observance of general laws' (11.17 / 138–9) could prevent God from acting benevolently. Natural evils are caused by the physical laws of nature – floods and hurricanes are meteorological phenomena – and moral evils are similarly dependent on the laws of nature since 'the conjunction between motives and voluntary actions is as regular and uniform, as that between the cause and effect in any part of nature' (8.16 / 88). Evil would therefore be unavoidable if God did not have control over these laws. The Christian God, though, does have such control: he is omnipotent and, as we saw in the discussion of miracles, he allegedly has the power to suspend the laws of nature. A Christian, therefore, cannot avoid the problem of evil by appealing to such laws.

Second, it has been argued that the world is better for containing evil. One reason for this is that certain human virtues can only be manifest if there is evil in the world. If there were no pain then we could not feel sympathy or compassion for our fellows. Such virtues are intrinsically good and, if we are assessing whether a certain world is better than another, their presence 'cancels out' the evils to which they are a response. A world containing pain and compassion is better than a world that contains neither.

> Every physical ill, say they, makes an essential part of the benevolent system, and could not possibly be removed, even by the Deity himself, considered as a wise agent, without giving entrance to greater ill, or excluding greater good, which will result from it . . . [T]hose ills, under which they laboured, were, in reality, goods to the universe; and that to an enlarged view, which could comprehend the whole system of nature, every event became an object of joy and exultation. (8.34 / 101)

There are various problems with this response. First, such an 'enlarged view' is no consolation to those who are suffering.

> You would surely more irritate, than appease a man, lying under the racking pains of the gout, by preaching up to him the rectitude of those general laws, which produce the malignant humours in his body . . . (8.34 / 101)

This thought is all the more pressing if larger-scale horrors are considered. Can we really say that our virtuous response to the Holocaust cancels out its evil, and that it is better for the world to include such evil (and its concomitant good) than not? However large one's view, the Holocaust could not become 'an object of joy and exultation'. Also, although it is true that many cases of suffering elicit virtuous responses in others; many do not. People die in agony and alone, with no one there to act kindly or with sympathy or compassion. Such suffering could be eliminated by an omnipotent God without reducing the amount of virtuous human behaviour in the world. Lastly, this attempt to avoid the problem of evil seems to clash with the Christian ideal of a future state. There – in heaven – all evil *is* eliminated.

A third theodicy focuses on free will. Actions can only be considered evil if they are performed freely. Human freedom, however, is intrinsically good and, as with the virtues above, its existence compensates for any evils that are a product of its exercise. A world containing freedom and freely chosen evil acts is better than a world that contains neither. (This approach only seems to counter moral evil, but some have argued that natural evils are caused by the free actions of fallen angels. Hume, I suspect, would claim that such an account strays into 'fairy land' as there is no empirical evidence to support it.)

The free-will response to the problem of evil is addressed by Hume at the end of his discussion of liberty and necessity (Section 8). Hume is a compatibilist: morally significant actions are both free and necessitated. An evil act is therefore the result of a long sequence of necessitated events. I kick the cat because I want to cause it pain; this desire is caused by my dislike of cats, which in turn is caused by my Mother's overindulgence of the family pet, and so on. This chain of causes ultimately leads back to God, the creator of the world. Thus:

> The Ultimate Author of all our volitions is the Creator of the world, who first bestowed motion on this immense machine, and placed all beings in that particular position, whence every subsequent event, by an inevitable necessity, must result. (8.32 / 99–100)

If this is so, the believer faces a dilemma.

> Human actions, therefore, either can have no moral turpitude at all, as proceeding from so good a cause; or if they have any turpitude, they must involve our Creator in the same guilt . . . (8.32 / 100)

Neither of these options is easy to accept. It would be 'absurd' to say that none of our actions is evil since God is ultimately their author; sceptical philosophical arguments cannot subvert our everyday moral reasoning to that extent. And, it would be 'impious' to ascribe evil acts to God, and this is certainly not a route that could be taken by a Christian. (Libertarians would argue that human action is not necessitated – it is metaphysically free – and thus its origin cannot be traced back to God; it arises only from the soul of individual moral subjects. Hume, however, has rejected such a conception of freedom.)

Hume ends this section seemingly perplexed about how this dilemma is to be resolved.

> These are mysteries, which mere natural and unassisted reason is very unfit to handle; and whatever system she embraces, she must find herself involved in inextricable difficulties, and even contradictions, at every step which she takes with regard to such subjects . . . Happy, if she be thence sensible of her temerity, when she pries into these sublime mysteries; and leaving a scene so full of obscurities and perplexities, return, with suitable modesty, to her true and proper province, the examination of common life; where she will find difficulties enow to employ her enquiries, without launching into so boundless an ocean of doubt, uncertainty, and contradiction! (8.36 / 103)

Much of the mystery here only arises if one believes in a Deity. Hume does not – this final comment does not express heartfelt modesty that a coherent theodicy is beyond mere human wisdom; it is, rather, another dig at religion: perhaps things would be less mysterious if we accepted a secular mechanistic view of morality and the world.

It is claimed by the theodicies above that the best of all possible worlds contains evil. This is either because God's providence is limited or because evil is necessarily accompanied by certain human virtues and free will. Lastly, though, Hume considers a rather different kind of approach. The evil we find in the world only indicates that progress is still to be made – progress, though, that is part of God's design plan: God may have created the world so that it progresses towards perfection in the future.

> If you saw, for instance, a half-finished building, surrounded with heaps of brick and stone and mortar, and all the instruments of masonry; could you not *infer* from the effect, that it was the work of design and contrivance? And could you not return again, from this inferred cause, to infer new additions to the effect, and conclude, that the building would soon be finished, and receive all the further improvements, which art could bestow upon it? . . .

> Consider the world and the present life only as an imperfect building, from which you can infer a superior intelligence; and arguing from that superior intelligence, which can leave nothing imperfect; why may you not infer a more finished scheme or plan, which will receive its completion in some distant point of space and time? (11.24 / 143)

On discovering an unfinished building we would be led to infer the existence of both a designer and a builder. An unfinished world should lead us to the same conclusion.

There is, however, a disanalogy between these two scenarios: between a half-finished building and a half-finished world there is an 'infinite difference of the subjects' (11.25 / 143). We have experienced the work of architects and builders; we know that their constructions take time, that they are sometimes left unfinished, and that they are sometimes shoddy. An unfinished house can therefore be taken as good empirical evidence that people have been involved in its construction. The knowledge we have of our own working practices allows such an inference to be made. We do not, however, have knowledge of the working practices of God; such an inference would therefore involve going beyond the empirical evidence.

> Man is a being, whom we know by experience, whose motives and designs we are acquainted with, and whose projects and inclinations have a certain connexion and coherence, according to the laws which nature has established for the government of such a creature . . . The Deity is known to us only by his productions, and is a single being in the universe, not comprehended under any species or genus, from whose experienced attributes or qualities, we can, by analogy, infer any attribute or quality in him. (11.25–6 / 143–5)
>
> It must evidently appear contrary to all rules of analogy to reason, from the intentions and projects of men, to those of a Being so different, and so much superior. (11.27 / 146)

If it is assumed that God exists, then we can infer that his world is unfinished and that his mature creation will come to fruition some time in the future. This inferred 'new effect' – a perfect world – provides us with all the more reason to believe in God. This, however, is not sound reasoning.

> We can never be allowed to mount up from the universe, the effect, to JUPITER, the cause; and then descend downwards, to infer any new effect from that cause; as if the present effects alone were not entirely worthy of the glorious attributes, which we ascribe to that deity. The knowledge of the cause being derived solely from the effect, they must be exactly adjusted to each other. (11.14 / 137)
>
> We [cannot], by any rules of just reasoning, return back from the cause, and infer other effects from it, beyond those by which alone it is known to us. (11.13 / 136)

We should only believe in the kind of creator necessary to produce the kind of world that we experience, and the world we currently inhabit does not call for the existence of a supremely good God.

> You afterwards become so enamoured of this offspring of your brain, that you imagine it impossible, but he must produce something greater and more perfect than the present scene of things, which is so full of ill and disorder. You forget, that this superlative intelligence and benevolence are entirely imaginary, or, at least, without any foundation in reason . . . Let your gods, therefore, O philosophers, be suited to the present appearances of nature . . . (11.15 / 137–8)

Theodicies attempt to show how evil is compatible with the existence and design plan of God. Thus, if there is good reason to think that the Christian deity exists, then attempts could be made to explain away the evil and misfortune that we find in the world. Hume's claim, though, is that there is no reason to believe in God in the first place and thus evil does not have to be explained away.

d. Causal inference and constant conjunction

The argument from design appears to have the following form. We know that man-made objects are the product of human design and manufacture. The universe as a whole bears certain analogies to such artefacts and thus we infer that its cause must also have been an intelligent designer. Hume ends this section by claiming that such reasoning cannot be applied to God's alleged creation of the universe. We saw in Section 7 that our knowledge of causes and effects – of what causes what – comes wholly from experience. We know that heat is an effect of fire because in our experience heat and fire have

been constantly conjoined. Consequently, we can only class something as an effect if it is the kind of thing that is constantly conjoined
with a certain kind of cause.

> When one particular species of event has always, in all instances,
> been conjoined with another, we make no longer any scruple of
> foretelling one upon the appearance of the other, and of employ-
> ing that reasoning, which can alone assure us of any matter of
> fact or existence. We then call the one object, *Cause*; the other,
> *Effect*. (7.27 / 74–5)

We have not, though, experienced lots of worlds being made. In our
experience worlds are not constantly conjoined with any antecedent
events and thus we cannot conceive of the world as an *effect* of anything.

> It is only when two *species* of objects are found to be constantly
> conjoined, that we can infer the one from the other; and were an
> effect presented, which was entirely singular, and could not be
> comprehended under any known *species*, I do not see, that we
> could form any conjecture or inference at all concerning its cause.
> (11.30 / 148)

It cannot therefore be argued that God exists using causal inference
as the argument from design attempts to do.

Hume could also argue in this way against modern versions of the
argument from design. For the universe to be as ordered as it is, and
for it to sustain intelligent life, a very specific set of natural laws must
be in operation. If these laws had been slightly different, then the
universe would have turned out chaotic and inhospitable. Swinburne
(1968) argues that the probability of just these laws coming about by
chance is extremely small. There must, therefore, be a reason why it
is these laws that govern the universe despite the incredible odds
against this being so. That reason is God; he fixed the dice; he
designed the universe to be this way. Hume's response to this line of
argument would be that probabilistic reasoning cannot be applied
here. Such reasoning is used when the empirical evidence falls short
of constant conjunction. I can infer that the next orange I eat will be
sweet, not because they always are, but because they mostly have
been in the past. Importantly, though, such reasoning requires

repeated experiences; no sense can be made of the probability of a unique event occurring. Probabilistic reasoning cannot therefore be applied to the creation of the universe.

e. Agnostic or atheist?

Hume is certainly anti-Christian: in Sections 10 and 11 he provides arguments against both the traditional supports for religious belief, against revealed and natural religion, and throughout these sections he inveighs against 'superstition' (Catholicism) and 'enthusiasm' (religious fanaticism). Buckle (2001) calls the *Enquiry* 'An Enlightenment Tract': it is a revolutionary call to adopt empirical scientific principles and in so doing reject a religious outlook on the world, Christian or otherwise. In the *Enquiry* the fundamental importance of his attack on religion becomes clear and his naturalistic, secular conception of our place in the world comes into focus. For prudential reasons his views have to be disguised but, as in the section on miracles, the rather mischievous phrasing of parts of Section 11 reveals much about his attitude towards religion. Flew (1961: 217) calls Hume's phrase, 'the religious hypothesis', 'piquantly provocative', and it is. In Hume's day 'hypothesis' referred to unwarranted speculation rather than, as it does today, to respectable scientific theory.

A corollary of Hume's rejection of religion is that man's existence has no great significance: 'the life of man is of no greater importance to the universe than that of an oyster' (Hume 1996a: 319). There is no God to intervene in our lives and to be a moral guide.

> I deny a providence, you say, and supreme governor of the world, who guides the course of events, and punishes the vicious with infamy and disappointment, and rewards the virtuous with honour and success, in all their undertakings. (11.20 / 140)

And there is no heaven and hell.

> [We have no reason to think that] this life [is] merely a passage to something farther; a porch, which leads to a greater, and vastly different building; a prologue, which serves only to introduce the piece, and give it more grace and propriety. (11.21 / 141)

There is therefore no particular providence or future state.

It does not follow, however, that Hume is an atheist in the modern sense, i.e. someone who explicitly believes that there is no supernatural power of any kind at work in the universe. To allow for such a possibility would certainly be consistent with Hume's general sceptical approach: without justified reasoning either for or against the existence of such a Being, we should suspend judgement on such matters. And various quotations both in the *Enquiry* and in his *Dialogues Concerning Natural Religion* could be seen to suggest such an 'agnostic' viewpoint.

> The cause, or causes, of order in the universe probably bear some remote analogy to human intelligence. (Hume 1779: 227)
> But this method of reasoning can never have place with regard to a Being, so remote and incomprehensible, who bears much less analogy to any other being in the universe than the sun to a waxen taper . . . (11.27 / 146)

Any such concession, though, does not provide shelter for any form of recognizable *religion* or for belief in a deity that has spacial concern for our welfare. Hume is consistently hostile to any such world view.

To those of a different temperament all of this could be terribly disconcerting, but not to Hume. His rejection of religion reveals much about his character, and his short autobiographical note, 'My Own Life', includes an inspiring example of how a non-believer should meet death.

> I have suffered very little pain from my Disorder; and what is more strange, have, notwithstanding the Great Decline of my Person, never suffered a Moments Abatement of my Spirits: Insomuch, that were I to name the Period of my Life which I should most choose to pass over again I might be tempted to point to this later Period. I possess the same Ardor as ever in Study, and the same Gaiety in Company.' (Hume 1776: 615)

Such contentment does not indicate a mellowing of his views on religion; he remained critical of Christianity until the end. In his final days he joked to a friend, the economist Adam Smith, about what he would say to Charon, the boatman of classical mythology, who takes the dying over the River Styx to Hades.

Have a little patience, good Charon, I have been endeavouring to open the eyes of the Public. If I live a few years longer, I may have the satisfaction of seeing the downfall of some of the prevailing systems of superstition. (Norton 1993: 23)

Questions

1. It is transparently obvious that the world was not created by the God of Christianity because such a God would not have allowed there to be the Holocaust or the Asian tsunami. Is this right?

2. Concerning religion, Hume says that 'our line is too short to fathom such immense abysses' (7.24 / 72). Discuss the various readings there could be of this claim. Hume's comment could, for example, be taken as one that is (i) agnostic towards religious belief; (ii) sceptical with respect to our epistemic abilities; or (iii) ironic. Which reading do you think best captures Hume's attitude?

3. How would Hume reply to the following?

Should it not astound me that anyone . . . can persuade himself . . . that a world of the utmost splendour and beauty is created by an accidental combination of [particles]? I do not see how the person who supposes that this can happen cannot also believe that if countless instances of the twenty-one letters were thrown into a container, then shaken out onto the ground, it were possible they might form a readable version of the *Annals* of Ennius. I'm not sure that luck could manage this to the extent of a single line! (Cicero, *De Natura Deorum*, 2.37; quoted in Gaskin 1993: 325)

4. If it is true that life on Earth has evolved through natural selection, what effect does this have on the argument from design?

12. OF THE ACADEMICAL OR SCEPTICAL PHILOSOPHY

a. The radical nature of Hume's scepticism

When we looked at Hume's treatment of causal reasoning in Section 4, we noted that Hume holds that all our beliefs about matters of fact that are not based on our memories or our present perceptual experiences are the products of causal reasoning. Moreover, we provisionally came to the conclusion that Hume denies that the conclusions arrived at by means of causal reasoning are rationally justified. This means, then, that we are already implicitly committed to thinking of Hume as someone who embraces a wide-ranging scepticism about the availability of rationally justified beliefs. What would the implications be if we found ourselves under pressure to attribute to Hume an even more extensive scepticism about rational justification? Would we have to conclude at that point that Hume's philosophical position is ultimately a deeply incoherent one? Would we need instead to reconsider the supposition that Hume holds that causal reasoning is unable to confer rational justification on its conclusions? Or is there some way of exhibiting global or near-global scepticism about the availability of rationally justified beliefs as a liveable and philosophically defensible position?

Fortunately Section 12 of the *Enquiry* proves to be of great assistance in resolving these questions. At the beginning of this section, Hume explicitly undertakes to inquire into the topic of what it means to describe someone as a sceptic, and how far it is possible 'to push these philosophical principles of doubt and uncertainty' (12.2 / 149). Moreover, Hume's investigations seem to lead to the identification of a form of scepticism that he is prepared to endorse as his own personal position.

The form of scepticism that Hume has in mind here is one he refers to as 'a more *mitigated* scepticism, or ACADEMICAL philosophy' (12.24 / 161). This should not really strike the attentive reader of the *Enquiry* as surprising. When Hume gives his response in Section 5 to his critique of causal reasoning in the immediately preceding section, he sets out this response under the highly significant title of 'Sceptical Solution of these Doubts'. Moreover, the scepticism introduced to the reader and defended against some common slanders is specifically picked out as 'the ACADEMICAL or SCEPTICAL philosophy' (5.1 / 41). Hume does not spell out at that point the details of this position, nor does he make any systematic attempt to distinguish it from other possible forms of scepticism. However, this omission is one that is remedied in the section we are now considering. And careful examination of the basis on which Hume recommends Academic scepticism, and his treatment of the relationship between such scepticism and Pyrrhonean scepticism, seems to reveal that Hume holds that the epistemological arguments employed by sceptics about rational justification are not only unanswerable but are also capable of indirectly influencing people's patterns of thought in a potentially beneficial way.

Academic scepticism is often thought of today as equivalent to an epistemological fallibilism that accepts that we can have rationally justified beliefs about a great many topics although we are unable to be absolutely certain that any of these beliefs are true. Richard Popkin, for example, gives the following account of Academic scepticism in *The History of Scepticism from Erasmus to Spinoza*:

> The Academic sceptics said that nothing is certain. The best information we can gain is only probable and is to be judged according to probabilities. Hence Carneades developed a type of verification theory and a type of probabilism which is somewhat similar to the theory of scientific 'knowledge' of present day pragmatists and positivists. (1979, xiv)

It also seems clear that an interpretation of this kind was widely accepted by Hume's contemporaries. We can see this by looking at a work by Jean Pierre de Crousaz that was translated into English as *A New Treatise of the Art of Thinking* in 1724 while Hume was a student at Edinburgh. We find that Crousaz reports that the Academics purported to find some things probable whereas the Pyrrhonists took the more extreme view that no judgement about any matter of inquiry is ever better justified than the opposite judgement:

> But there are some Persons, who affect to remain in Uncertainty, and seem to be afraid of getting out of it. These are sometimes called Academics, because the Philosophers, who seemed to incline to this universal Doubting, taught in a House called the Academy . . . They are also called Sceptics, from a Greek word that signifies to consider; because instead of judging rashly, they loved to examine a Thing on all Sides. At last Pyrrhon, one of the most famous Advocates of this Sect, gave his Name to it . . . The Sceptics, in looking for Certainty, set a value on Probability; but the Pyrrhonians would not own one Proposition to be more probable than another. Indeed how could they say, that a Proposition is probable and comes near the Truth, when they maintained that the Mind of Man has no idea of Truth, and does not know the Character of it. (1724: Pt. 2, 119)

Significantly, however, it does not seem possible to treat Hume's own talk about Academic scepticism as similarly equivalent to talk about modest epistemological fallibilism. If we were to attempt such an interpretation, then the fact that Section 12 of the *Enquiry* sees Hume repeatedly contrasting this form of scepticism with a position picked out by the term 'PYRRHONISM, or excessive scepticism' (12.24 / 161) could leave us in no doubt that Hume views Pyrrhonism as a more extreme form of scepticism that not only denies that any of our beliefs are certainly true, but also maintains that very few of our beliefs even manage to be rationally justified. It follows that if Hume is to hold that large numbers of our everyday beliefs are rationally justified, he must be of the opinion that one can sincerely deny that the arguments put forward by Pyrrhonean sceptics are rationally compelling arguments while simultaneously affirming that many of one's own beliefs are rationally justified. Yet the only criticism to be found in the *Enquiry* of the Pyrrhonist's arguments is the claim that we cannot expect any durable good or social benefit to result from these arguments while their force remains unchecked by the power of our natural instincts.

It seems clear, therefore, that the particular form of Academic scepticism endorsed by Hume cannot be correctly categorized as the view that many of our beliefs are rationally justified though none is certainly true. If many of our beliefs are rationally justified, then some of the premises of the Pyrrhonist's arguments must be false or there must be flaws in his inferences. Now the charge that the Pyrrhonist's arguments suffer from defects of these kinds would obviously be a more philosophically pertinent and damaging objection than the allegation that his arguments do nothing to further human happiness. But, as we have just noted, the latter objection is the only one Hume chooses to raise. Indeed, he explicitly refers to it as the principal objection that can be brought against radical scepticism.

> For here is the chief and most confounding objection to *excessive* scepticism, that no durable good can ever result from it; while it remains in its full force and vigour. We need only ask such a sceptic, *What his meaning is? And what he proposes by all these curious researches?* He is immediately at a loss, and knows not what to answer. (12.23 / 159–60)

Thus the conspicuous absence from Hume's text of any deeper criticism strongly suggests that Hume is actually convinced that the radical sceptic is correct in claiming that scarcely any of our beliefs are ever rationally justified.

b. The causal origins of Hume's Academic scepticism

Once we have decided that the Academic scepticism endorsed by Hume is not the view that we can have rationally justified beliefs but are precluded from having certain knowledge, we might be momentarily at a loss to understand what it is that he is endorsing. After all, if Hume genuinely believes that the Pyrrhonean sceptic's epistemological arguments are unanswerable, why does he not openly endorse Pyrrhonean scepticism?

Fortunately, it is possible to infer from the way that Hume sets out his own stance that the Academic scepticism he favours is a state of mind that he believes emerges spontaneously and naturally when the psychological mechanisms that generate our beliefs are forced to interact with the conviction that very few, if any, of our beliefs are capable of being rationally justified. This conviction is one that can, in Hume's judgement, be induced by thoughtful reflection on the arguments employed by Pyrrhonists; but it is incapable of completely overriding the psychological processes that sustain our everyday beliefs about the existence and properties of such things as trees, tables and clouds. On the other hand, it does tend to make us appreciably more diffident about the truth of our opinions:

> The greater part of mankind are naturally apt to be affirmative and dogmatical in their opinions . . . But could such dogmatical reasoners become sensible of the strange infirmities of human understanding, even in its most perfect state, and when most accurate and cautious in its determinations; such a reflection would naturally inspire them with more modesty and reserve, and diminish their fond opinion of themselves, and their prejudice against antagonists. (12.24 / 161)

And Hume also holds that it protects us against our propensity to theorize about topics that lie entirely beyond human experience:

> A correct *Judgment* . . . confines itself to common life, and to such subjects as fall under daily practice and experience; leaving

the more sublime topics to the embellishment of poets and orators, or to the arts of priests and politicians. To bring us to so salutary a determination, nothing can be more serviceable than to be once thoroughly convinced of the force of the PYRRHONIAN doubt, and of the impossibility, that any thing, but the strong power of natural instinct, could free us from it. (12.25 / 162)

Hume's own position, then, is not the product of a recognition of deficiencies in the case for widespread scepticism about rational justification. There are, in his judgement, no such deficiencies to be discovered. The arguments that can be brought forward in support of the view that no beliefs about the existence of mind-independent objects are rationally justified are, he believes, unanswerable. Similarly, the case for supposing that causal reasoning cannot confer justification on its conclusions is as strong a piece of reasoning as it is possible to construct. And the existence of paradoxes relating to infinity and infinite divisibility is presented by Hume as potentially subverting the supposition that the methods of investigation employed within arithmetic and geometry are capable of generating rationally defensible beliefs.

What actually allows Hume to combine a generous stock of beliefs with his appreciation of the plausibility of such sceptical arguments is the sustaining power of natural instinct and the vivacity inherent in perceptual impressions. These sub-rational psychological mechanisms causally suffice to hold in place most of our beliefs even when we are confronted by unanswerable sceptical arguments. And this phenomenon also provides Hume with his defence to the charge that he ought to abandon all the beliefs he sees as lacking rational justification.

It seems fairly plausible to suppose that one cannot be under an obligation to perform a task that is beyond one's powers. At the most one can only be under an obligation to attempt the task in question. Moreover, it is not legitimate to suppose that what a person can do sometimes, and in some conditions, he can do at all times and in all conditions. Hence someone who purports to give his sincere assent to negative epistemological arguments of the kind found in the *Enquiry* and elsewhere in Hume's writings can admit that it is sometimes possible to suspend belief in response to the apparent discovery that a belief is unjustified, and yet deny that it is possible for him to suspend belief on all occasions when he comes to the conclusion that no rational grounds for belief are present. And if this is impossible, perhaps due to the biological and psychological constitution possessed by human beings, then it cannot be the case that he ought to eschew all those beliefs that strike him as lacking any rational justification.

It is also important to keep in mind here the difference in psychological condition between someone who genuinely believes that none of our beliefs within a particular domain of discourse can ever possess any rational justification, and someone who holds that it is possible to reach justified beliefs within that domain. Consequently it cannot legitimately be argued that if an ordinary person could succeed in suspending belief on a given topic, it must also be psychologically possible for a sincere advocate of the negative epistemological arguments presented in the *Enquiry* to suspend belief. The ordinary person presumably retains a real hope that either he or someone else will ultimately be able to arrive at a justified belief concerning that topic, and he might well be very reluctant, accordingly, to do anything that strikes him as likely to obstruct or delay the emergence of such a belief. Thus the ordinary person confronted by an inclination to acquiesce in a belief despite its lack of rational justification has a substantial incentive to resist that inclination that would rarely, if ever, be available to someone who endorses the epistemological arguments that concern us here. And it seems plausible to suppose that the absence of this particular incentive would lead to such a person finding that there are circumstances in which he is utterly unable to resist forming beliefs in accordance with his natural inclinations, even though an ordinary person would have been able to force himself to suspend judgement in those same circumstances. We are, therefore, free to think of the person who genuinely endorses negative epistemological arguments of the kind set out in the *Enquiry* as being involuntarily pushed into beliefs by psychological forces that might potentially be resistible, e.g. by someone who could call upon the mental energies made available by a commitment to the view that succumbing to such inclinations would significantly reduce his opportunities to acquire rationally justified beliefs.

At the same time, however, it is important to keep in mind that the shock of confronting sceptical arguments about rational justification and coming to recognize our inability to answer them is not wholly devoid of its own causal consequences. The causal power of natural instinct and lively impressions generally dominates, but sceptical arguments can sweep away beliefs that are not founded on such sources. The impact of such arguments also has just sufficient effect on more deeply entrenched beliefs to make us more diffident about our opinions and more modest in our inquiries. Thus the mitigated or Academic scepticism advocated by Hume comes into existence as the product of the interaction between two causal forces: perception and natural instinct on the one hand, and the psychological impact of a set of unanswerable arguments on the other. As a result of this interaction we find ourselves in the useful and congenial psychological posture Hume calls Academic scepticism, but we do not relinquish the philosophical belief that very few, if any, of our beliefs possess any positive degree of rational justification.

c. Scepticism and inquiry

How, then, will an Academic sceptic conduct his inquiries? He will generally refrain from thinking of one claim as better justified than another. However, that will not prevent him from being influenced by his impressions and the associative mechanisms that come to link one idea with another. When those factors are working in an unimpeded fashion, his beliefs about matters of truth and falsity will be both strong and stable. Moreover, there is no basis for supposing that the Academic sceptic will eschew all complicated forms of scientific and philosophical reasoning. In many cases such reasoning is simply a more systematic and methodical application of modes of belief-formation that naturally command our allegiance and invigorate our ideas. Where this is so, the Academic sceptic will tend to arrive at the same non-epistemic beliefs as his non-sceptical colleagues.

In situations where philosophy and science cease to be systematized common sense and take on loftier pretensions, the outcome will be very different. The beliefs generated in these cases are not properly supported by a transfer of vivacity from perception and experiment. Instead, they are sustained only by a much looser association of ideas in the imagination, and processes of education or propaganda lead to fanciful suggestions being received by impressionable minds as though they were supported by weighty evidence. Hume is confident, accordingly, that refined sceptical reasoning can often suffice to disrupt these loose associations. And this, in turn, clears the way for the results of observation and experiment to have a real opportunity to overturn the results of false and inappropriate teaching.

The conclusion of the *Enquiry* is not, therefore, a confession of the need to suspend belief or abandon our critical faculties. Hume does admittedly drive home repeatedly the message that rational justification as conceived of by philosophers and those influenced by them is generally, perhaps even always, beyond our reach. He fully accepts that the force of Pyrrhonean doubt is such that no arguments can show it to be mistaken: it can be held in check only by 'the strong power of natural instinct' (12.25 / 162). However, this is simply part of the overall picture. Even as we accept that the sceptical arguments against the availability of justification are unanswerable, we continue to inquire and make inferences in the way dictated to us by the natural psychological mechanisms that hold sway in the human mind. Indeed, those psychological mechanisms now work in an even more stable and predictable way. This is because reflection on those sceptical arguments helps to eliminate the distractions and false opinions generated by those associative links that are not firmly grounded in the relation between cause and effect.

The upshot is actually a more consistent and determined form of empiricism, at least at the level of belief, than anything espoused by Hume's non-sceptical contemporaries. Someone who embraces Academic scepticism as a result of becoming conscious of the lack of justification for most of his beliefs does undergo a transformation that leaves him less dogmatic and more willing to listen to others. However, he also becomes more reliant on the invigorating influence of impressions and the strong associative links generated by the kind of constant conjunctions in experience that underpin our causal inferences. So although he is perfectly capable of continuing to learn from the latest teachings of those scientists and other thinkers who genuinely rely on experience and experiment rather than armchair theorizing, the crucial difference in respect of his attitude to profound and complicated reasoning lies in his increased intolerance of theories that lack that kind of experiential support.

It is in this way that Hume arrives at his dramatic conclusion:

If we take in our hand any volume; of divinity or school metaphysics, for instance; let us ask, *Does it contain any abstract reasoning concerning quantity or number?* No. *Does it contain any experimental reasoning concerning matter of fact and existence?* No. Commit it then to the flames: For it can contain nothing but sophistry and illusion. (12.34 / 165)

From Hume's perspective, only reasoning of the two types he has just identified can sustain stable beliefs in the face of sceptical arguments and unprejudiced encounters with the results of observation and well-directed experiments. Anyone rash enough to disdain those two sources of belief will simply find that his opinions are pulled apart by the power of sceptical arguments. But the result of confining our beliefs to these two sources of impressions and lively ideas is that the dramatic edifices constructed by theologians and non-sceptical metaphysicians spectacularly collapse under their own weight because of their lack of foundations in permanent aspects of human psychology.

Questions

1. Would it be credible to maintain that Hume's apparent scepticism is merely a device for exposing the inadequacies of a particular understanding of what constitutes rational justification rather than a serious attempt to maintain that scarcely any of our beliefs ever possess any genuine justification?

2. Is Hume's 'Academic philosophy' simply rampant Pyrrhonism repackaged under a less alarming label?

3. How plausible is Hume's attempted reconciliation of respectable scientific practice with scepticism?

4. If we reviewed the *Enquiry* according to Hume's own principles, would we find ourselves condemning it to the flames along with those metaphysical treatises that Hume accuses of containing nothing other than 'sophistry and illusion'?

CHAPTER 5

HUME'S INFLUENCE

1. THE EPISTEMOLOGY OF TESTIMONY

Hume is a key influence on social epistemology and particularly on the debate concerning testimonial knowledge. In epistemology the word 'testimony' has a broad application: it refers to the everyday occurrences of when we find something out from somebody else; discussions of testimony do not simply concern the formal testimony given in a law court or the religious testimony given in a chapel. Testimonial reports can be comprised of the spoken or written word, mime, semaphore and all the other forms of communication that we use to pass on information about the world.

It is unavoidable that many of our beliefs are acquired via testimony, although philosophers have traditionally seen the pursuit of *knowledge* as a solitary activity. This is true of both the rationalist and empiricist traditions: an individual thinker acquires knowledge for herself either through a priori reasoning or through empirical reasoning grounded in perception. On this 'individualistic' approach I may come to acquire beliefs from others, but these do not amount to knowledge until I have checked for myself whether they are true. Such beliefs are second hand *and* second rate. Here is Locke expressing this position.

I hope it will not be thought arrogance to say, that perhaps we should make greater progress in the discovery of rational and contemplative knowledge if we sought it in the fountain, in the consideration of things themselves, and made use rather of our own thoughts than other men's to find it: for, I think, we may as rationally hope to see with other men's eyes as to know by other men's understanding . . . The floating of other men's opinions in our brains makes us not one jot the more knowing, though they happen to be true. What in them was science is in us but opiniatrety. (Locke 1689: I.IV.23)

And here is a modern philosopher concurring with the individualistic approach.

No doubt, we all do pick up beliefs in that second-hand fashion, and I fear that we often suppose such scavengings yield knowledge. But that is only a sign of our colossal credulity: [it is] a rotten way of acquiring beliefs and it is no way at all of acquiring knowledge. (Barnes 1980: 200)

Recently, however, there has been considerable interest in moving away from the individualistic conception of knowledge; it is claimed that we *can* acquire knowledge from others. We should note that this certainly chimes with how we generally talk about knowledge. The response to the question, 'How do you know that?' is often: 'Somebody told me so', 'I saw it on the TV' or 'I read it in a book'. And some putative examples of testimonial knowledge include the claim that the number 50 bus goes to Druids Heath (I have never stayed on the bus past Kings Heath and so I have not checked for myself whether this is true); the vegetarian lasagne does not contain nuts (I was not present when it was made); human beings have brains (I have never looked inside anyone's skull); and my birthday is 4 February (I have taken my parents' word for this). It is certainly true that such testimonial beliefs are widespread, and that we have no option but to rely on them; we simply do not have the time to check out the veracity of all such beliefs for ourselves. The key question, though, is whether we can acquire knowledge, and not merely belief, via testimony.

Hume has become central to this debate. He was one of the first philosophers to note the importance of testimony:

There is no species of reasoning more common, more useful, and even necessary to human life, than that which is derived from the testimony of men, and the reports of eye-witnesses and spectators. (10.5 / 111)

After we have acquired a confidence in human testimony, books and conversation enlarge much more the sphere of one man's experience and thought than those of another. (9.5, fn. 20 / 107, fn.)

And he suggests an account of how our testimonial beliefs can amount to knowledge.

> It will be sufficient to observe, that our assurance in any argument of this kind [argument 'derived from the testimony of men'] is derived from no other principle than our observation of the veracity of human testimony, and of the usual conformity of facts to the reports of witnesses. It being a general maxim, that no objects have any discoverable connexion together, and that all the inferences, which we can draw from one to another, are founded merely on our experience of their regular and constant conjunction . . . (10.5 / 111)

Hume has been taken to recommend an 'inferential' account of testimonial knowledge. I should only believe what someone says if I know that they have a good track record, that is, if I know that they have reliably told the truth before. In the past Scott has always been right about how the stock markets are performing. I should therefore believe him when he tells me the NASDAQ has fallen today. Testimonial knowledge is based on past experience: 'past conformity of facts to the reports of witnesses' leads me to continue to believe that the reports of such witnesses are reliable. We have seen that, for Hume, such reasoning is not *justified*; it is, however, preferred to other kinds of thinking – such as those based on religious enthusiasm and faith – not because we can provide rational argument to support it, but because this is the kind of everyday reasoning that we habitually pursue. From the perspective of everyday life, sceptical philosophical arguments are impotent in the face of our customary ways of thinking.

> The reason why we place any credit in witnesses and historians, is not derived from any *connexion*, which we perceive *a priori*, between testimony and reality, but because we are accustomed to find a conformity between them. (10.8 / 113)

Hume's account is problematic in various ways. In most cases we have not collected enough evidence in order to make the necessary inferences. I am shocked by certain events that I hear about on the news tonight. On Hume's account, though, it is not clear whether I should believe what the newsreader says. I have never heard him speak before, and thus, I have no knowledge of his past record. There is also a problem with respect to science. Scientists engage in collaborative work: pooling equipment, skills, research grants and, importantly, data. For Hume, though, a scientist should only accept the data of a colleague if she herself has evidence that this colleague's data has been accurate in the past. An individual scientist, however, simply does not have the time or a sufficiently wide range of skills to determine whether this is so.

In response to such problems there is the 'fundamentalist' approach to testimony, an approach influenced by Thomas Reid, a contemporary of Hume. Reid argues that we should always accept someone's testimony unless we have good reason to suspect that a particular report is false. The default position is one of trust, and this does seem to fit with our actual practice: generally we just believe what people say unless we have good reason not to. Debate between the followers of Hume and Reid dominates the philosophical discussion of testimony, one of the hot issues in contemporary epistemology. Hume notes the importance of testimony and argues that it should only be accepted if we are able to check that our informants have been reliable in the past. There is therefore an individualistic aspect to Hume's approach. Testimony may provide us with knowledge – something that Locke denies – but only if we have acquired substantial empirical information about our informants. Reid rejects this strand of individualism: we have a prima facie right to accept testimony whether or not we have evidence concerning a speaker's past record. It is important to note, though, that followers of Hume and Reid share a key commitment: knowledge *can* be acquired via testimony. Testimonial knowledge may be 'second-hand' – it is knowledge that at some time must have been acquired by others – but it is not second rate.

2. NATURALIZED EPISTEMOLOGY

Throughout we have seen that Hume recommends a distinctly naturalistic approach to epistemology and to the science of man, and this important strand in his thinking is very influential on both contemporary epistemology and the philosophy of mind. A naturalized approach to epistemology is one that is driven by the findings of empirical science. Traditional epistemology has focused on the problem of justification, and Hume has argued that we cannot have justified beliefs about the future, the unobserved or causal powers. Quine, however, has claimed that the whole justificatory framework should be abandoned, and that 'traditional philosophical problems are not meant to be solved' (1985: 465). Instead, we should undertake an altogether different approach to questions concerning our knowledge of the world.

> The stimulation of his sensory receptors is all the evidence anybody has to go on, ultimately, in arriving at his picture of the world. Why not just see how this construction really proceeds? Why not settle for psychology? (Quine 1969: 75–6)

Quine claims that we should aim to give a scientific account of how we come to have the beliefs that we do. We should not consider whether these beliefs are *justified*. All that is required is a causal description of our belief-forming mechanisms, and this causal story will be informed by the work of cognitive scientists, neurophysiologists and those working in evolutionary biology. Naturalized epistemologists should be interested in how biological creatures like us come to represent the state of their environment, and what cognitive mechanisms are involved in processes such as belief formation, perception and memory. 'Epistemology is best looked upon . . . as an enterprise within natural science' (Quine 1975: 68).

Both Quine and Hume acknowledge that sceptical doubts cannot be refuted by philosophical argument: 'The Humean predicament is the human predicament' (Quine 1969: 72). And, in the face of such scepticism, Hume also provides a genetic account of how we are caused to have the beliefs that we do. He does not provide justification for our empirical beliefs; instead, with his principles of association, he offers a rudimentary associative psychology which describes the regular flux of ideas in our mind. For both Hume and the naturalized epistemologist, the methods of epistemology are empirical. We should note the subtitle of Hume's *Treatise* (1739–40): 'An Attempt to Introduce the Experimental Method of Reasoning into Moral Subjects'. (Given Quine's basically Humean standpoint, his professed attitude to lecture-giving is somewhat uncharitable: 'Determining what Hume thought and imparting it to students was less appealing than determining the truth and imparting that' – Quine 1985: 194.)

Quine finds a metaphor of Otto Neurath's instructive.

> I see philosophy not as an a priori groundwork for science, but as continuous with science. I see philosophy and science as in the same boat – a boat which, to revert to Neurath's figure as I so often do, we can rebuild only at sea while staying afloat in it. There is no external vantage point, no first philosophy. (Quine 1969a: 126–7)

If we are interested in improving our sailing, we do not question the nature of buoyancy. Instead, we look to refine our sailing techniques by finding more and more sophisticated ways of using the equipment on board the boat. Analogously, when empirically investigating the world, we should not question whether the practice of science is justified; instead, we should simply continue to construct more and more sophisticated scientific theories of how the world and our cognition proceed.

Epistemology, though, is not simply concerned with what we happen to believe; its main interest would seem to be in what we should believe, or what we are entitled to believe. The latter are called 'normative' questions, and Quine acknowledges that these are some of the questions that epistemologists should attempt to answer.

> Naturalism not only consigns the question of reality to science; it does the same for normative epistemology. The normative is naturalized, not dropped . . . It is natural science that tells us that our information about the world comes only through impacts on our sensory surfaces. And it is conspicuously normative, counselling us to mistrust soothsayers and telepathists. (Quine in Barrett and Gibson 1990: 229)

Through empirical investigation of the world we come to discover that only some of our methods of belief acquisition are reliable. We rightly conclude that experimental science should be pursued and that telepathy should not. This is akin to Hume's recommendation of empirical reasoning over that tainted with, for example, 'the love of wonder'. We may not be able to provide philosophical argument to show that such reasoning is *justified*, but it is nevertheless the kind of thinking that we should pursue when judged from the perspective of everyday life.

Quine claims that traditional epistemology is redundant. In contrast, other naturalistically minded epistemologists accept that traditional epistemology poses the right questions; these are questions, though, that must be answered using the resources of science. Such naturalists do not eschew the philosophical notion of justification; instead, they attempt to give a scientific account of the nature of this epistemic property. Their naturalism does not involve a rejection of traditional philosophy, but rather, the claim that scientific practice should feed into the traditional philosophical debate.

> The results from the sciences of cognition may be relevant to, and may be legitimately used in the resolution of traditional epistemological problems. (Haack 1993: 118)

Some naturalists explain justification in terms of the causal relations that there are between thinkers and the world: a justified belief that one is eating an orange is one that is caused in the right kind of way by an orange. Justification is therefore explained in terms of properties that are scientifically respectable. Such accounts may pose their own problems, but they remain within the domain of traditional epistemology. Importantly, though, they are also clearly 'an attempt to introduce the experimental method of reasoning into moral subjects', and thus, they have been influenced by Hume's vision of epistemology.

3. COGNITIVE SCIENCE

The philosophy of mind is central to Hume's account of human nature even though this was not, at the time, seen as a distinctive subject. After giving an inventory of the contents of the mind in terms of ideas and impressions, and an account of how these are related together through the principles of association, he then goes on to explain how this cognitive architecture gives rise to the ideas of causation, morality, and free will. And, Hume is a naturalist: he argues that the mind should be studied in the same way as other natural phenomena, that is, by the 'experimental method'. In the eighteenth century this was a radical approach; we are akin to animals and turnips, and not to God. This, however, has now become the orthodox approach to the philosophy of mind, and this is in good part due to Hume.

Hume conjectures that minds obey certain psychological laws (a fact that he nevertheless sees as compatible with our having free will), and he comes to this conclusion both through observing the 'common course of the world, by men's behaviour in company, in affairs, and in their pleasures' (1739–40: xix), and through introspection of his own mental states. The modern discipline of cognitive science can be seen as embracing Hume's experimental method and as attempting to provide an account of our mental states and of the laws that they obey.

> It becomes, therefore, no inconsiderable part of science barely to know the different operations of the mind, to separate them from each other, to class them under their proper heads, and to correct all that seeming disorder, in which they lie involved . . . [This is a] mental geography or delineation of the distinct parts and powers of the mind . . . (1.13 / 13)

In the *Treatise* Hume acknowledges Newton as a great influence: his theory of gravity providing the seed for Hume's own mechanical theory of the imagination. Mechanism was not new: Newton provided a mechanistic account of nature, and Descartes that of the body. Hume, however, extended this approach to the mind, and he was therefore centuries ahead of his time. (Newton and Descartes did not consider a mechanistic account of the mind because of their Christian views, views that we have seen Hume rejects.)

Jerry Fodor, a leading cognitive scientist, cites Hume as an influence.

> Hume's *Treatise* is the foundational document of cognitive science: it made explicit, for the first time, the project of constructing an empirical psychology on the basis of a representational theory of the mind. (Fodor 2003: 134)

According to Fodor, Hume develops a theory of the mind that treats mental processes as involving causal interaction between what are now called 'mental representations' (Hume's ideas and impressions). And this is the correct approach to take:

> The main reason I've cared about Hume's account of the mind was that it seems, in a number of respects, to anticipate the one that informs current work in cognitive science. (Fodor 2003: 2)

However, Hume's philosophy of mind appears in various ways very different from the kinds of theories put forward by contemporary

naturalists, and consequently his influence on today's scene is somewhat obscured. First, his associative psychology is very crude and
unable to account for the nature of thought. Fodor and many others
agree that Hume is highly influential on today's naturalistic
approach, but everyone also agrees that the principles of association
should not have a central role in a theory of cognition. 'The foundations of modern, empirical, cognitive science is indeed part of the
legacy of Hume the philosopher, but not of Hume the psychologist'
(Millican 2002: 52).

Second, the metaphysics required to sustain Hume's idea theory
leads to a position that contemporary naturalists reject. Hume
appears to accept Descartes' dualist ontology: the body may be
physical, but the mind consists in non-physical ideas or images.
Today's naturalists are wedded to materialism and to the view that
the mind is wholly physical. There are, however, suggestions of this
approach in Hume. The association of ideas depends on the movement of animal spirits – these 'spirits' could perhaps be seen as physical nerve impulses – and these physiological phenomena may
depend on deeper physical regularities.

> We learn from anatomy, that the immediate object of power in
> voluntary motion, is not the member itself which is moved, but
> certain muscles, and nerves, and animal spirits, and, perhaps,
> something still more minute and more unknown, through which
> the motion is successively propagated . . . (7.14 / 66)

Elsewhere, Hume's wording also suggests that he may be willing to
give up dualism:

> Is there any principle in all nature more mysterious than the union
> of soul with body; by which a *supposed* spiritual substance acquires
> such an influence over a material one, that the most refined thought
> is able to actuate the grossest matter? (7.11 / 65; our emphasis)
>
> Is there not here, either in a spiritual *or material substance*, or
> both, some secret mechanism or structure of parts, upon which
> the effect depends, and which, being entirely unknown to us,
> renders the power or energy of the will equally unknown and
> incomprehensible? (7.19 / 68–9; our emphasis)
>
> [Thought is the] offspring of your brain. (11.15 / 137)

To this day there are echoes of the problems Hume had in reconciling his naturalistic approach with the introspective evidence. Hume was a committed naturalist and advocated a causal account of the mind. He could not, though, see any alternative to thinking of mental states as ideas or images. His philosophy of mind therefore takes these as given; ideas themselves are not explained in causal terms, although his causal account provides a description of how such mental items are related together. Opponents of today's naturalistic approach focus on just the kind of first-person evidence that, for Hume, reveals the mind as consisting of more or less vivid ideas and impressions. Cognition has a certain phenomenology – it feels like something to have certain mental states – and causal accounts cannot provide a persuasive story of why this should be so. *What it is like* to look at the blue sky and to feel pain is not explainable in terms of the 'material substance' of the brain. This tension between the subjective evidence – Hume's ideas, and today's 'feels' or 'qualia' – and an objective causal account is still very acute in today's philosophy of mind.

Cognitive science is now an interdisciplinary research programme that brings together workers in psychology, computer science, neurophysiology, linguistics, evolutionary biology and philosophy. Such disciplines did not exist in Hume's day and therefore Hume is not a cognitive scientist in our sense. He is, however, an important precursor to this whole movement. It is not too fanciful to claim that Hume would have looked very favourably on this modern approach to the mind, and, if he were around today, one can easily see him as a director of a cognitive science programme rather than as a professor of metaphysics or traditional epistemology. His philosophy does include a great deal of psychology; and this may be amenable to the computational approach: according to Flew, Hume sees thought as the 'automatic . . . operation of a sort of experiential computing machine' (Flew 1961: 212); his talk of 'animal spirits' suggests an interest in neurophysiology; and it is not hard to imagine Hume embracing a Darwinian evolutionary account of life and of the mind.

CHAPTER 6

FURTHER READING

1. NOTES ON THE TEXT

The edition of the *Enquiry* that is most usually referred to is:

Hume, D. (1777) *Enquiries Concerning Human Understanding and Concerning the Principles of Morals*, ed. L. Selby-Bigge; revd P. Nidditch; Clarendon Press: Oxford, 1975.

There is also an excellent new edition which we suspect will become the standard:

Hume, D. (1772) *An Enquiry Concerning Human Understanding*, ed. T. Beauchamp; OUP: Oxford, 1999.

An electronic version is at:

www.etext.leeds.ac.uk/Hume/

And some libraries will also hold the useful CD Rom:

Complete Works & Correspondence of David Hume, Intelex Corporation, Charlottesville, Va. www.nlx.com

2. SECONDARY LITERATURE ON THE *ENQUIRY*

Buckle, S., (2001) *Hume's Enlightenment Tract: The Unity and Purpose of* An Enquiry Concerning Human Understanding, OUP: Oxford.

Flew, A., (1961) *Hume's Philosophy of Belief: A Study of His First 'Inquiry'*, Routledge & Kegan Paul: London.

Millican, P. (ed.), (2002) *Reading Hume on Human Understanding: Essays on the First* Enquiry, OUP: Oxford.

Penelhum, T., (1992) *David Hume: An Introduction to his Philosophical System*, Purdue University Press: Lafayette, Ind.

Stern, G., (1971) *A Faculty Theory of Knowledge: The Aim and Scope of Hume's* First Enquiry, Bucknell University Press: Lewisburg, Pa.

3. SECONDARY LITERATURE ON HUME'S PHILOSOPHY

Dicker, G., (1998) *Hume's Epistemology and Metaphysics*, Routledge: London.

Garrett, D., (1997) *Cognition and Commitment in Hume's Philosophy*, OUP: Oxford.

—— (2005) 'Hume' in the *Routledge Encyclopedia of Philosophy* <http://www.rep.routledge.com>.

Kemp Smith, N., (1941) *The Philosophy of David Hume*, Macmillan: London.

Noonan, H., (1999) *Hume on Knowledge*, Routledge: London.

Norton, D. F. (ed.), (1993) *The Cambridge Companion to Hume*, CUP: Cambridge.

Noxon, J., (1973) *Hume's Philosophical Development*, Clarendon Press: Oxford.

Owen, D. (ed.), (2000) *Hume: General Philosophy*, Ashgate: Aldershot.

Passmore, J., (1980) *Hume's Intentions*, 3rd edn, CUP: Cambridge.

Pears, D., (1990) *Hume's System*, OUP: Oxford.

Stewart, M. and J. Wright (eds), (1994) *Hume and Hume's Connexions*, Edinburgh University Press: Edinburgh.

Stroud, B., (1977) *Hume*, Routledge & Kegan Paul: London.

Tweyman, S. (ed.), (1995) *David Hume: Critical Assessments*, 6 vols, Routledge: London.

Hume Studies journal published biannually in April and November.

4. DETAILED FURTHER READING

Chapter 1. Context

Box, M.A., (1990) *The Suasive Art of David Hume*, Princeton University Press: Princeton.

Buckle, S., (2001) *Hume's Enlightenment Tract*, OUP: Oxford.

Burton, J.H., (1846) *Life and Correspondence of David Hume*, Tait: Edinburgh.

Greig, J.Y.T., (1931) *David Hume*, OUP: Oxford.

Millican, P., (2002) 'The Context, Aims, and Structure of Hume's First *Enquiry*' in Millican (2002) 27–65.

Mossner, E.C., (1980) *The Life of David Hume*, 2nd edn, OUP: Oxford.

Stern, G., (1980) *A Faculty Theory of Knowledge: The Aim and Scope of Hume's* First Enquiry, Bucknell University Press: Lewisburg, Pa.

Chapter 2. Sources

Annas, J. and J. Barnes, (1985) *The Modes of Scepticism*, CUP: Cambridge.

Brush, C., (1966) *Montaigne and Bayle: Variations on the Theme of Skepticism*, Martinus Nijhoff: The Hague.

Cottingham, J., (1988) *The Rationalists*, OUP: Oxford.

Fogelin, R.J., (2001) *Berkeley and the* Principles of Human Knowledge, Routledge: London.

Hankinson, R.J., (1995) *The Sceptics*, Routledge: London.

Jones, P., (1982) *Hume's Sentiments: Their Ciceronian and French Context*, Edinburgh University Press: Edinburgh.

Kuypers, M.S., (1930) *Studies in the Eighteenth Century Background of Hume's Empiricism*, University of Minnesota Press: Minneapolis.

Labrousse, E., (1983) *Bayle*, OUP: Oxford.

Lennon, T.M., (1999) *Reading Bayle*, University of Toronto Press: Toronto.

Lowe, E.J., (1995) *Locke on Human Understanding*, Routledge: London.

McCracken, C.J., (1983) *Malebranche and British Philosophy*, OUP: Oxford.

Mossner, E.C., (1980) *The Life of David Hume*, 2nd edition, OUP: Oxford.

Noxon, J., (1973) *Hume's Philosophical Development*, OUP: Oxford.

Popkin, R.H., (1980) *The High Road to Pyrrhonism*, ed. R.A. Watson and J.E. Force; Austin Hill Press: San Diego.

Stewart, M.A. (ed.), (1990) *Studies in the Philosophy of the Scottish Enlightenment*, OUP: Oxford.

Urmson, J.O., (1982) *Berkeley*, OUP: Oxford.

Woolhouse, R.S., (1983) *Locke*, Harvester Press: Brighton.

—— (1988) *The Empiricists*, OUP: Oxford.

Yolton, J.W. (1993) *A Locke Dictionary*, Blackwell: Oxford.

Chapter 3. Overview of themes
1. Empiricism

Aune, B., (1970) 'The Paradox of Empiricism', *Metaphilosophy*, 1: 128–38.

Bennett, J., (1971) *Locke, Berkeley, Hume*, OUP: Oxford.

Mackie, J.L., (1976) *Problems from Locke*, OUP: Oxford.

Macnabb, D.G.C., (1966) *David Hume: His Theory of Knowledge and Morality*, Basil Blackwell: Oxford.

Pears, D., (1990) *Hume's System*, OUP: Oxford.

Price, H.H., (1940) *Hume's Theory of the External World*, OUP: Oxford.

Yolton, J.W., (1964) 'The Concept of Experience in Locke and Hume', *Journal of the History of Philosophy*, 1: 53–71.

Zabeeh, F., (1973) *Hume: Precursor of Modern Empiricism*, Martinus Nijhoff: The Hague.

2. Epistemological scepticism

Bailey, A., (1989) 'Rediscovering Scepticism', *Eidos*, 8: 153–76.

—— (2002) *Sextus Empiricus and Pyrrhonean Scepticism*, OUP: Oxford.

Fogelin, R.J., (1983) 'The Tendency of Hume's Skepticism' in M. Burnyeat (ed.), *The Skeptical Tradition*, University of California Press: Berkeley.

—— (1985) *Hume's Skepticism in the* Treatise of Human Nature, Routledge & Kegan Paul: London.

Livingston, D.W. (1984) *Hume's Philosophy of Common Life*, University of Chicago Press: Chicago.

Norton, D.F., (1984) *David Hume: Common-Sense Moralist, Sceptical Metaphysician*, Princeton University Press: Princeton.

Popkin, R.H., (1951) 'David Hume: His Pyrrhonism and His Critique of Pyrrhonism', *Philosophical Quarterly*, 1: 385–407.

Robison, W.L., (1976) 'David Hume: Naturalist and Meta-Sceptic' in D.W. Livingston and J.T. King (eds), *Hume: A Re-evaluation*, Fordham University Press: New York, 23–49.

Williams, B. (1983) 'Descartes' Use of Scepticism' in M. Burnyeat (ed.), *The Skeptical Tradition*, University of California Press: Berkeley, 337–52.

Williams, M., (2001) *Problems of Knowledge*, OUP: Oxford.

3. A naturalistic account of human beings
Buckle, S., (2001) *Hume's Enlightenment Tract*, OUP: Oxford.
Craig, E., (1987) *The Mind of God and the Works of Man*, OUP: Oxford.
Kemp Smith, N., (1941) *The Philosophy of David Hume*, Macmillan: London.
Stroud, B., (1977) *Hume*, Routledge & Kegan Paul: London.
Wright, J.P., (1983) *The Sceptical Realism of David Hume*, Manchester University Press: Manchester.

4. Secularism
Berman, D., (1988) *A History of Atheism in Britain: From Hobbes to Russell*, Routledge: London.
Craig, E., (1997) *Hume on Religion*, Indian Institute of Advanced Study: Shimla.
Gaskin, J.C.A., (1988) *Hume's Philosophy of Religion*, 2nd edn, Macmillan Press: Basingstoke.
—— (1993) 'Hume on Religion' in D. F. Norton (ed.), *The Cambridge Companion to Hume*, CUP: Cambridge, 313–4
Noxon, J., (1964) 'Hume's Agnosticism', *Philosophical Review*, 73: 248–61.
O'Connor, D. (2001) *Hume on Religion*, Routledge: London.

Chapter 4. Reading the text

1. Of the different species of philosophy
Box, M.A., (1990) *The Suasive Art of David Hume*, Princeton University Press: Princeton.
Buckle, S., (2001) *Hume's Enlightenment Tract*, OUP: Oxford.
Stewart, M.A., (2002) 'Two Species of Philosophy: The Historical Significance of the First *Enquiry*' in P. Millican (ed.), *Reading Hume on Human Understanding*, OUP: Oxford, 67–95.

2. Of the origin of ideas
Anderson, R.F., (1966) *Hume's First Principles*, University of Nebraska Press: Lincoln.
Bennett, J., (2002) 'Empiricism about Meanings' P. Millican (ed.), *Reading Hume on Human Understanding*, OUP: Oxford, 97–106.
Bricke, J., (1980) *Hume's Philosophy of Mind*, Edinburgh University Press: Edinburgh.
Craig, E., (1986) 'Hume on Thought and Belief' in G. Vesey (ed.) *Philosophers Ancient and Modern*, CUP: Cambridge, 93–110.
Govier, T., (1972) 'Variations on Force and Vivacity in Hume', *Philosophical Quarterly*, 22: 44–52.
Macnabb, D.G.C., (1966) *David Hume: His Theory of Knowledge and Morality*, Basil Blackwell: Oxford.
Pears, D., (1990) *Hume's System*, OUP: Oxford.
Stroud, B., (1977) *Hume*, Routledge and Kegan Paul: London.
Waxman, W., (1994) *Hume's Theory of Consciousness*, CUP: Cambridge.

3. Of the association of ideas
Biro, J., (1993) 'Hume's New Science of the Mind' in D. F. Norton (ed.) *The Cambridge Companion to Hume*, CUP: Cambridge, 33–63.
Buckle, S., (2001) *Hume's Enlightenment Tract*, OUP: Oxford.
Passmore, J., (1980) *Hume's Intentions*, 3rd edition, Duckworth: London.
Wright, J.P., (1983) *The Sceptical Realism of David Hume*, Manchester University Press: Manchester.

4. Sceptical doubts concerning the operations of the understanding
Blackburn, S. (1973) *Reason and Prediction*, CUP: Cambridge.
Dicker, G., (1998) *Hume's Epistemology and Metaphysics*, Routledge: London.
Fogelin, R.J., (1985) *Hume's Skepticism in the* Treatise of Human Nature, Routledge & Kegan Paul: London.
Garrett, D. (1997) *Cognition and Commitment in Hume's Philosophy*, OUP: Oxford.
Millican, P., (2002) 'Hume's Sceptical Doubts Concerning Induction' in P. Millican (ed.), *Reading Hume on Human Understanding*, OUP: Oxford, 107–74.
Morris, W.E., (1988) 'Hume's Refutation of Inductive Probabilism' in J.H. Fetzer (ed.), *Probability and Causality*, Reidel: Dordrecht,
Noonan, H., (1999) *Hume on Knowledge*, Routledge: London.
Skyrms, B., (1986) *Choice and Chance*, 3rd edn, Wadsworth: Belmont, California.
Stroud, B., (1977) *Hume*, Routledge and Kegan Paul: London.
Winkler, K., (1999) 'Hume's Inductive Skepticism' in M. Atherton (ed.) *The Empiricists*, Rowman and Littlefield: Lanham, Maryland.

5. Sceptical solution of these doubts
Bell, M., (2002) 'Belief and Instinct in Hume's First *Enquiry*' in P. Millican (ed.), *Reading Hume on Human Understanding*, OUP: Oxford, 175–86.
Bell, M. and M. McGinn, (1990) 'Naturalism and Scepticism', *Philosophy*, 65: 399–414.
Capaldi, N., (1975) *David Hume: The Newtonian Philosopher*, Twayne: Boston.
Fogelin, R.J., (1985) *Hume's Skepticism in the* Treatise of Human Nature, Routledge and Kegan Paul: London.
Strawson, P.F., (1985) S*kepticism and Naturalism*, Methuen: London.
Stroud, B., (1977) *Hume*, Routledge & Kegan Paul: London.

6. Of probability
Gower, B., (1991) 'Hume on Probability', *British Journal for the Philosophy of Science*, 42: 1–19.
Hacking, I., (1978) 'Hume's Species of Probability', *Philosophical Studies*, 33: 21–37.

7. The idea of necessary connection
Beauchamp, T. and A. Rosenberg, (1981) *Hume and the Problem of Causation*, OUP: Oxford.

Craig, E., (2002) 'The Idea of Necessary Connexion' in P. Millican (ed.), *Reading Hume on Human Understanding*, OUP: Oxford, 211–230.

Lesher, J., (1973) 'Hume's Analysis of Cause and the "Two Definitions" Dispute', *Journal of the History of Philosophy*, 11: 387–92.

Mackie, J., (1974) *The Cement of the Universe*, Clarendon Press: Oxford.

Read, R. and K. Richman (eds), (2002) *The New Hume Debate*, Routledge: London.

Strawson, G., (1989) *The Secret Connexion*, Clarendon Press: Oxford.

—— (2002) 'David Hume: Objects and Power' in P. Millican (ed.), *Reading Hume on Human Understanding*, OUP: Oxford, 231–258.

Wright, J., (1983) *The Sceptical Realism of David Hume*, Manchester University Press: Manchester.

8. Of liberty and necessity

Botterill, G., (2002) 'Hume on Liberty and Necessity' in P. Millican (ed.), *Reading Hume on Human Understanding*, OUP: Oxford, 277–300.

Bricke, J., (1988) 'Hume, Freedom to Act, and Personal Evaluation', *History of Philosophy Quarterly*, 5: 141–56. Reprinted in S. Tweyman (ed.), (1995) *Hume*, vol. 4: 175–191.

Hobart, R., (1934) 'Free-Will as Involving Determination and Inconceivable Without It', *Mind*, 43: 1–27.

Honderich, T., (1993) *How Free Are You?*, OUP: Oxford.

Russell, P., (1995) *Freedom and Moral Sentiment*, OUP: Oxford.

Turgman S. (ed.) (1995) *David Hume: Critical Assessments*, Routledge: London: Vol. 4, 175–9.

Vesey, G. 'Hume on Liberty and Necessity' in G. Vesey (ed.), (1986) *Philosophers Ancient and Modern*, CUP: Cambridge: 111-27.

Watson, G. (ed.), (1982) *Free Will*, OUP: Oxford.

9. Of the reason of animals

Arnold, D., (1995) 'Hume on the Moral Difference Between Humans and Other Animals', *History of Philosophy Quarterly*, 12: 303–16.

Baier, A., (1985) 'Knowing Our Place in the Animal World' in *Postures of the Mind: Essays on Mind and Morals*, University of Minnesota Press: Minneapolis.

Dawkins, M., (1998) *Through Our Eyes Only?*, OUP: Oxford.

Huxley, T., (1886) *Hume*, Macmillan: London, ch. 5, 'The Mental Phenomena of Animals'.

Pitson, A., (1993) 'The Nature of Humean Animals', *Hume Studies*, 19: 301–16.

10. Of miracles

Broad, C., (1916–17) 'Hume's Theory of the Credibility of Miracles', *Proceedings of the Aristotelian Society*, 17: 77–94.

Burns, R., (1981) *The Great Debate on Miracles*, Associated University Presses: London.

Earman, J., (2000) *Hume's Abject Failure: The Argument Against Miracles*, OUP: Oxford.

Flew, A., (1959) 'Hume's Check', *Philosophical Quarterly*, 9: 1–18.

Fogelin, R.J. (2003) *A Defense of Hume on Miracles*, Princeton University Press: Princeton.

Garrett, D., (2002) 'Hume on Testimony Concerning Miracles' in P. Millican (ed.), *Reading Hume on Human Understanding*, OUP: Oxford, 301–334.

Houston, J., (1994) *Reported Miracles: A Critique of Hume*, CUP: Cambridge.

Johnson, D., (1999) *Hume, Holism, and Miracles*, Cornell University Press: Ithaca, NY.

Levine, M., (1989) *Hume and the Problem of Miracles*, Kluwer: Dordrecht.

Mackie, J., (1982) *The Miracle of Theism*, Clarendon Press: Oxford.

Swinburne, R., (1970) *The Concept of a Miracle*, Macmillan: London.

Tweyman, S. (ed.), (1996) *Hume on Miracles*, Thoemmes Press: Bristol.

11. Of a particular providence and of a future state

Adams, M. and R. Adams, (eds), (1990) *The Problem of Evil*, OUP: Oxford.

Flew, A. (ed.), (1992) *David Hume: Writings on Religion*, Open Court: La Salle, Ill.

Gaskin, J., (1988) *Hume's Philosophy of Religion*, MacMillan: London.

—— (2002)'Religion: The Useless Hypothesis' in P. Millican (ed.), *Reading Hume on Human Understanding*, OUP: Oxford, 349–70.

Swinburne, R., (1968) 'The Argument From Design', *Philosophy*, 43: 199–212.

—— (1979)*The Existence of God*, Clarendon Press: Oxford.

Yandell, K., (1990) *Hume's 'Inexplicable Mystery': His Views on Religion*, Temple University Press: Philadelphia.

12. Of the Academical or sceptical philosophy

Bailey, A., (2002) *Sextus Empiricus and Pyrrhonean Scepticism*, OUP: Oxford.

Buckle, S., (2001) *Hume's Enlightenment Tract*, OUP: Oxford.

Fogelin, R.J., (1983) 'The Tendency of Hume's Skepticism' in M. Burnyeat (ed.), *The Skeptical Tradition*, University of California Press: Berkeley.

Groarke, L., (1990) *Greek Scepticism: Anti-Realist Trends in Ancient Thought*, McGill-Queen's University Press: Montreal and Kingston.

Hookway, C., (1990) *Scepticism*, Routledge: London.

Norton, D.F., (1984) *David Hume: Common-Sense Moralist, Sceptical Metaphysician*, Princeton University Press: Princeton.

—— (2002) 'Of the Academical or Sceptical Philosophy' in P. Millican (ed.), *Reading Hume on Human Understanding*, OUP: Oxford, 371–92.

Popkin, R.H., (1951) 'David Hume: His Pyrrhonism and His Critique of Pyrrhonism', *Philosophical Quarterly*, 1: 385–407.

Stroud, B., (1991) 'Hume's Scepticism: Natural Instincts and Philosophical Reflection', *Philosophical Topics*, 19: 271–91.

Tweyman, S., (1974) *Scepticism and Belief in Hume's* Dialogues Concerning Natural Religion, Martinus Nijhoff: The Hague.

BIBLIOGRAPHY

(Publication details of all books mentioned in the text)

Bailey, A. (2002) *Sextus Empiricus and Pyrrhonean Scepticism*, OUP: Oxford.

Barfoot, M. (1990) 'Hume and the Culture of Science in the Early Eighteenth Century' in M. Stewart (ed.), *Studies in the Philosophy of the Scottish Enlightenment*, OUP: Oxford: 151–90.

Barnes, J. (1980) 'Socrates and the Jury', *Proceedings of the Aristotelian Society*, suppl. vol. 54: 193–206.

Barrett, R. and R. Gibson (eds) (1990) *Perspectives on Quine*, Blackwell: Oxford.

Bayle, P. (1991) *Historical and Critical Dictionary: Selections*, trans. R.H. Popkin; Hackett Publishing Company: Indianapolis.

Bennett, J. (1971) *Locke, Berkeley, Hume*, OUP: Oxford.

Broad, C. (1916–17) 'Hume's Theory of the Credibility of Miracles', *Proceedings of the Aristotelian Society*, 17: 77–94.

Buckle, S. (2001) *Hume's Enlightenment Tract: The Unity and Purpose of* An Enquiry Concerning Human Understanding, OUP: Oxford.

Byrne, R. and A. Whiten (1988) *Machiavellian Intelligence: Social Expertise and the Evolution of the Intellect in Monkeys, Apes and Humans*, Clarendon Press: Oxford.

Cheney, D. L. and R. M. Seyfarth (1985) 'Social and Non-Social Knowledge in Vervet Monkeys', *Philosophical Transactions of the Royal Society of London, B*, 308: 187–201.

Clutton-Brock, T. H. and S. D. Albon (1979) 'The Roaring of Red Deer and the Evolution of Honest Advertisement', *Behaviour*, 69: 145–70.

Crousaz, J.P. de (1724) *A New Treatise of the Art of Thinking*, Tho. Woodward: London.

Darwin, C. (1859) *The Origin of Species by Means of Natural Selection*, John Murray: London.

Dawkins, M. (1993) *Through Our Eyes Only? The Search for Animal Consciousness*, W. H. Freeman and Company Ltd: New York.

Descartes, R. (1984) *Meditations on First Philosophy* in *The Philosophical Works of Descartes*, Vol. II, trans. J. Cottingham, R. Stoothoff and D. Murdoch; CUP: Cambridge.

Diderot, D. (1955) *Correspondance*, Vol. I, ed. G. Roth and J. Varloot; Editions de Minuit, Paris.

Everson, S. (1995) 'The Difference between Feeling and Thinking' in S. Tweyman (ed.), *David Hume: Critical Assessments*, Vol. 1, Routledge: London.

Flew, A. (1961) *Hume's Philosophy of Belief: A Study of His First 'Inquiry'*, Routledge & Kegan Paul: London.

Fodor, J. (2003) *Hume Variations*, Clarendon Press: Oxford.

Gaskin, J. (1993) 'Hume on Religion' in Norton (ed.) 1993: 313–44.

Haack, S. (1993) *Evidence and Inquiry: Towards Reconstruction in Epistemology*, Blackwell: Oxford.

Hartley, D. (1749) *Observations on Man, his Frame, his Duty, and his Expectations*, vols, S. Richardson: London.

Hume, D. (1739–40) *Treatise of Human Nature*, ed. L. Selby-Bigge; 2nd edn, revd P. Nidditch, Clarendon Press: Oxford, 1978.

—— (1972) *An Enquiry Concerning Human Understanding*, ed. T. Beauchamp; OUP: Oxford, 1999.

—— (1776) 'My Own Life' in Mossner 1980: 611–15.

—— (1777) *Enquiries Concerning Human Understanding and Concerning the Principles of Morals*, ed. L. Selby-Bigge; revd P. Nidditch; Clarendon Press, Oxford, 1975.

—— (1779) *Dialogues Concerning Natural Religion*, ed. N. K. Smith; Clarendon Press: Oxford; 2nd edn, Thomas Nelson & Sons, London, 1947.

—— (1932) *Letters of David Hume*, Vol. 1, ed. J.T.Y. Greig, OUP: Oxford.

—— (1964) 'Hume to Michael Ramsay, 31 August 1737'; in R. Popkin, *The Journal of Philosophy*, 61: 773–8.

—— (1983) *The History of England*, 6 vols, Liberty Fund: Indianapolis.

—— (1987) *Essays, Moral, Political, and Literary*, ed. E.F. Miller, Liberty Classics: Indianapolis.

—— (1993) 'A Kind of History of My Life'; in Norton (ed.) 1993.

—— (1996) 'Of the Immortality of the Soul' in *Selected Essays*, ed. S. Copley and E. Elgar; OUP: Oxford.

—— (1996a) 'Of Suicide' in *Selected Essays*, ed. S. Copley and E. Edgar; OUP: Oxford, 1996.

Kant, I. (1788) *Critique of Practical Reason*, trans. L. Beck; Bobbs-Merrill: Indianapolis, 1956.

Leibniz, G. (1705) *New Essays on Human Understanding*, ed. P. Remnant and J. Bennett; CUP: Cambridge, 1981.

Locke, J. (1689) *An Essay Concerning Human Understanding*, ed. P. Nidditch; Clarendon Press: Oxford, 1975.

Lovejoy, A. (1936) *The Great Chain of Being*, Harvard University Press: Cambridge, Mass.

Mackie, J. (1980) *The Cement of the Universe*, OUP: Oxford.

Malebranche, N. (1980) *The Search after Truth*, trans. T.M. Lennon and P.J. Olscamp; Ohio State University Press: Columbus.

Miller, R. E. (1971) 'Experimental Studies of Communication in the

Monkey' in *Primate Behaviour*, ed. L. A. Rosenblum; Vol. 2, Academic Press: New York: 113–28.

Millican, P. (ed.) (2002) *Reading Hume on Human Understanding: Essays on the First Enquiry*, OUP: Oxford.

Mossner, E. (1980) *The Life of David Hume*, 2nd edn, OUP: Oxford.

Newton, I. (2004) *Philosophical Writings*, ed. A. Janiak; CUP: Cambridge.

Norton, D. F. (ed.) (1993) *The Cambridge Companion to Hume*, CUP: Cambridge.

Popkin, R.H. (1979) *The History of Scepticism from Erasmus to Spinoza*, University of California Press: Berkeley.

Quine, W.U.O. (1969) 'Epistemology Naturalized?' in *Ontological Relativity and Other Essays*, Columbia University Press: New York: 69–90.

—— (1969a) 'Natural Kinds' in *Ontological Relativity and Other Essays*, Columbia University Press: New York: 114–38.

—— (1975) 'The Nature of Natural Knowledge' in S. Guttenplan (ed.) (1975), *Mind and Language*, Clarendon Press: Oxford.

—— (1985) *The Time of my Life*, Bradford Books and MIT Press: Cambridge, Mass.

Searle, J. (1984) *Minds, Brains and Science*, Penguin: Harmondsworth.

Sextus Empiricus (1933) *Outlines of Pyrrhonism* in *Sextus Empiricus*, trans. R.G. Bury; Volume 1 of 4; Harvard University Press: Cambridge, Mass.

Smith, P. and O.R. Jones (1986) *The Philosophy of Mind*, CUP: Cambridge.

Stove, D.C. (1973) *Probability and Hume's Inductive Scepticism*, OUP: Oxford.

Strawson, G. (1989) *The Secret Connexion: Causation, Realism and David Hume*, Clarendon Press: Oxford.

Stroud, B. (1977) *Hume*, Routledge & Kegan Paul: London.

Swinburne, R. (1968) 'The Argument From Design', *Philosophy*, 43.

Taylor, R. (1974) *Metaphysics*, Prentice-Hall, Inc.: Englewood Cliffs, NJ.

INDEX